Deeper into the Garden

the Garden

meditating with plants

JUDITH BROOKS

WITH

PAULETTE MILLICHAP

AND MEDITATIONS BY

AMELIA VOGLER

WITH ART BY

DODI O'NEILL

MILLICHAP BOOKS

www.deeperintothegarden.com

©2021 Judith Brooks. All rights reserved

Cover and interior artwork © 2020 by Dodi O'Neill
All rights reserved

Photos © 2021 Judith Brooks except where noted

First edition. First printing 2021

This book is not intended to give any medical advice on herbal medicine. Please seek the advice and care from a professional healthcare provider for all medical problems.

ISBN 978-1-937462-44-4

Cover and interior design by Carl Brune

With gratitude to the Goddesses Green Tara, Ixchel, and Quan Yin.

We have to get back to being in integration with the land, and then our thoughts are going to be in tune with environmental consciousness.

JOSEPH RAEL
Beautiful Painted Arrow (1935–)
Sound: Native Teachings & Visionary Art

Contents

Flower Essences 85

Herbal Basics and Recipes 95

Teachings from our Elders 105

Conclusion 113

Introduction

Being in nature, touching, smelling and sitting with plants calms and restores our mind and spirit. That we respond to this healing presence of plants is not surprising. That the plants respond to our attention by slowly revealing themselves is the simple miracle we want to share.

As we wrote this book, COVID-19 had become a pandemic, and many people globally face economic, environmental, and racial and social crises. These evolutionary stressors give us an opportunity to ask ourselves questions. Where do we find resilience and hope? How do we find balance and inner peace? How do we adapt to change?

We can choose to take a respite from our busy lives and go for a walk in nature or sit quietly outside with the plants and trees. We can begin to quiet our nervous system and deepen our connection with ourselves in the natural world. Being with plants and realizing their inherent intelligence helps us open new gateways of perception.

It is early spring in North Carolina and new rue leaves are emerging. The elder bush has hardy, purplish-green leaves sprouting from its branches. Rosemary has an abundance of periwinkle blue flowers. Nature teaches us about the state of impermanence. Like the seasons, life is constantly changing.

A deep yearning is pulling us toward something we can't quite name. What is this desire that's calling? Perhaps it is a longing to join with many who want to be in a right relationship with nature and with those who want to deepen their compassion and sense of peace in the natural world. Many people are feeling the call to create a new paradigm that includes respect for all living beings. We invite you to open your gates of perception and join us in the garden.

Entering the New Garden

If the doors of perception were cleansed everything would appear to man as it is, infinite.

WILLIAM BLAKE
English poet, 1757–1837

The Return

I came back to North Carolina in 2012, after living away for almost forty years, and moved back into my childhood home. I'm not sure what a ghost is, but since being home, I can hear my mother's voice. She loved plants and understood them in a deep way. I still remember her telling me to go out to the garden and to listen to the corn to hear what it needed. I came home to listen to the corn and to enter more deeply into communion with plants and the land where I grew up.

I have been the publisher of many Native American writers, especially Native elder Joseph Rael, known as Beautiful Painted Arrow. Grandfather Joseph had a vision in 1983 to build round, kiva-like structures in the earth where people could chant for the purity and health of the streams and rivers and oceans of the world. Joseph called these structures Sound Chambers. In his vision he was shown how to build chambers so the sound would be magnified like a singing bowl. Many of these chambers have been built around the world, and are used for chanting, ceremony, and prayer.

Since Joseph had told me there was a Sound Chamber nearby, I contacted the chamber caretaker and asked if I could come and visit. She gave me directions and invited me to join them for a Fire Ceremony. This ceremony is to honor and heal the waters of the earth, and it is held in chambers around the world at 7:00 p.m. on the seventh day of the month.

I was excited to meet a community of people that came together each month to pray for the healing of our planet. I was welcomed into the circle, and the fire was lit. We watched the fire in silence until the fire went out and we ended the ceremony with chanting.

Grandfather Joseph teaches us how to listen to the voice of Mother Earth, how to embody the wisdom of the earth, and how to dance with the earth and sing her songs. He teaches that everything is vibration.

After the ceremony, I started a conversation with a woman with dark, wavy hair who was sitting next to me. Her name was Judith and she told me she had been a student of Joseph's for many years and had read several of his books that I had edited and published. That one of Joseph's chambers existed close to the home where I grew up, and that I was meeting one of his students at this moment, was amazing to me. It was as if the many years of my publishing career had come full circle.

Paulette

A NEW GARDEN

THE NEXT WEEK, JUDITH INVITED ME TO VISIT HER GARDEN.
We shared some herbal tea and sat outside. Near us a beautiful
praying mantis sat on a holy basil plant, perfectly still as if it were
meditating. I have come to believe the praying mantis was carrying a
message. I feel it was teaching us to be still, go deeper, and listen.

Judith gave me a few holy basil plants to take home and told me
that holy basil, also known as tulsi, is a sacred plant in Hinduism and
blesses one's home. I held the small pot of holy basil as I sat on my
deck wondering where I could plant it. After living in the city for
many years, I had lost the ability to be comfortable out in nature.
When I looked closely at the dirt in my backyard, I saw how it was
full of feces, worms, slugs, and all kinds of other icky things I didn't
want to touch. Yet this dirt was the concentrated decay of everything
that had come before, never mind that this same dirt would be the
rich soil I needed to build a new garden.

I called Judith and asked her to come over. We stood near where
my mother's old garden had been and where I thought we might
put a new garden. Judith touched the ground and said, "There is
good soil under this grass." We decided to lay out the garden with a
compass and make it round like a medicine wheel to honor Joseph's
teachings and the four directions.

I was grateful that my son dug out the grass and prepared the soil
with compost. Now the new, circular garden was ready for seeds and
plants that we had found at a local nursery.

We planted the garden with calendula, borage, echinacea, thyme
and native perennials like joe-pye weed and milkweed. We watched
as the plants began to bloom in the sunshine. We were delighted
to see many pollinators such as bees, butterflies and hummingbirds
visiting. Judith told me that respect for the plants is important. We
can honor each plant for its medicine and beauty and approach each
plant as a friend.

PAULETTE IN HER GARDEN

Judith's words resonated with me because I had published books on gardening and books on healing with herbs and indigenous books on mystical relationships with animals, rocks and plants. I had published Joseph Rael and had heard him say all things are vibration. I knew and loved Joseph's stories about growing up at Picuris Pueblo in New Mexico, and especially loved his story about his grandmother telling him as a small boy to sit down and listen to the bowl singing.

In Joseph's Tiwa language, there are no nouns. In his language everything is a verb, alive and in motion. Joseph told me to step outside the western paradigm I grew up with where our language is divided into subject, object, and verb. He told me to see a world where everything is connected and dancing with everything else.

I was hungry to feel myself connected to the garden. I wanted the separation between myself and other living things to fall away. I wanted to experience each plant with the innocence of a child.

I GREW UP IN THE SUBURBS OF NEW JERSEY and both my parents, having lived through the era of the Great Depression, believed it was important to have a garden. My father grew up on a small apple farm in New York state, where his family had grown a lot of their own food. He liked to garden and when spring came to New Jersey, he would plant a vegetable garden in our small backyard. One of my childhood chores was to water the garden and harvest the vegetables. Both my Sicilian grandparents and my English grandmother had beautiful gardens. I am grateful for my early introduction to the wonderful world of plants.

I moved to upstate New York to go to college, and later moved to an organic farm that was also an intentional community. I was happy on the farm, where I had my hands in the earth, planting and tending to the crops. We grew a wide variety of vegetables and herbs for the farmers' market and local restaurants. I also was learning about homesteading and how to live with others in community.

My friend Joyce also lived on the farm and had a beautiful circular herb garden. I am grateful for her encouraging me on my herbal path. I helped her weed while she taught me about medicinal plants: how to dry herbs, harvest roots and blend teas. She also introduced me to the book called *Being and Vibration* by Joseph Rael, who later became an influential teacher in my life.

I became interested in learning more about healing and herbal medicine and decided to move to New Mexico, where I enrolled in acupuncture school. There was a herbal apothecary at the school, and I enjoyed putting together formulas for clients at the student clinic. In my free time I would wander in the desert, always amazed at the tenacity of the plants. I grew to love the desert but there was part of me that missed the green landscapes of the East Coast.

Since I had a few friends in North Carolina, I decided to move there after graduating from acupuncture school. In 1999 I moved cross-country with my dog, Golda. We found a rental house with a backyard for Golda to play and a place for planting a small garden. I made new friends who were also interested in herbs. We started meeting regularly for plant walks, learning to identify and study the native plants.

My passion for studying herbs has taken me on field trips to other countries where I have met indigenous healers. I learned about ethnobotany, which is the study of plants in relation to the culture and customs of the people who use the plants. I realized the elders who I met carried a precious oral tradition of plant medicine. Like the Amazon forest, some of this knowledge was disappearing as the elders passed. In Peru, I went on walks with healers who knew the plants to treat a snake bite, or how to treat a wound or an infection using plants, as a medical clinic could be hours away.

During a walk, I brushed against a palo santo tree and a fire ant bit my finger. It started to swell and throb with pain. The village healer leading our walk quickly picked a plant I didn't know, applied it to my finger, and told me it would bring the swelling down, which it did.

The fire ants have a symbiotic relationship with the tree. The palo santo's bark provides the ants a home while the ants keep the area around the tree free of vegetation and predators. My experience of the ant bite was an initiation, and it increased my awareness of plant intelligence and respect for those who carry the traditions of plant medicine.

I met Grandfather Joseph Rael at a gathering in the North Carolina mountains and became interested in sound healing after reading several of his books. I was honored to meet Grandfather Joseph in person and soon became a student of his. Joseph's teachings inspired me to chant to the plants in my garden as a way of connecting with them.

It was no coincidence that Paulette and I met at a ceremony that was connected to Grandfather Joseph. She asked me to help her plant a garden in her backyard. As the garden bloomed and grew, we began to sit quietly in her garden, appreciating the silence.

I had told Paulette about my travels to Belize and how I had felt connected to the land and people who lived there. In 2018, we had an opportunity to take an herbal immersion class with Dr. Rosita Arvigo and her co-teachers Eva and Toby Sengfelder and Trudy Zimmerly. Paulette and I traveled to Belize along with Paulette's two daughters and a family friend.

We spent time in the rainforest going on plant walks and immersing ourselves in the beauty of Rosita's gardens. We saw howler monkeys, parrots, and blue morpho butterflies. We were introduced to many medicinal plants. The class travelled to Eva and Toby Sengfelder's permaculture farm called Arco Iris, which is the home of Rainforest Remedies, Ltd., an herbal company dedicated to producing ethically-grown herbal formulas with plants from Belize. We participated in making herbal remedies from the plants on the farm.

Paulette and I continued to meet regularly to meditate in her garden. This book evolved out of our shared experiences and inspirations we received from our teachers, the plants.

ABOVE : LEFT TO RIGHT

JACKASS BITTERS, *Neurolaena lobata,* USED TO TREAT PARASITES, AMOEBAS AND FUNGUS.

POLLY RED HEAD, *Hamelia patens,* ALSO KNOWN AS "GUARDIAN OF THE FOREST" BY THE MAYA. USED TO TREAT SKIN CONDITIONS, SORES AND INSECT BITES.

HIBISCUS, *Hibiscus rosa-sinensis,* THIS IS A MEDICINAL EDIBLE FLOWER RICH IN IRON. FLOWERS ARE USED TO TREAT POSTPARTUM HEMORRHAGES, EXCESSIVE MENSTRUAL BLEEDING AND ANEMIA.

BELOW : LEFT : THE RAINFOREST IN BELIZE

BELOW : RIGHT : PAULETTE WITH DAUGHTERS DONNA AND KELLY IN BELIZE

Awakening Our Perceptions

e began our exploration in the garden by meditating with a plant, sometimes with our eyes closed, and sometimes with them open. We wrote our impressions of the plants in our journals. Each time we sat in the garden, we decided to be with a particular plant as our meditation partner for the day.

We would look at the plant carefully, counting the petals of its flowers, and noticing the shape of its leaves and the scent of its blossoms. Sometimes we used a magnifying device to look at all the tiny parts of the flowers. This opened a whole new world of exquisite detail and beauty.

We spent time sitting in the silence, feeling the sunlight on our skin, listening to the sounds the wind would make blowing through the leaves, listening to the buzzing of the bees, and watching the dance of the butterflies. We marveled at the plant's transformation through the seasons.

As we carefully touched a plant, we noticed whether it was velvety soft or had bristly stems or even thorns. We rolled the leaves in our fingers, releasing the aromatic scents, smelling the flowers and the leaves. Sometimes we would taste a plant and notice its complex flavors on our tongue. Many of the plants were bitter, others pungent, sour or sweet. Some plants are toxic, so we would only taste those we knew were safe.

As we meditated we became aware of an energy field that was emanating from the plants. We also became aware of expanded perceptions we were feeling in our bodies as we became more sensitive to the energy around each plant. We were attuning ourselves to the vibration of the plants.

Human beings have an innate ability to perceive energies in other beings, whether that being is a plant, an animal or a person. When we bring our attention to these sensations, another level of awareness becomes available to us. Using our intuition, we can interpret these sensations by giving each sensation an image or a feeling. In this way we are learning a new language that is beyond words.

As an acupuncturist who works with the body's energy fields, Judith recognized the sensations were similar to the ones used in healing. When we slowly passed our hands over a plant, we could feel warmth in our palms. Other times we felt a humming in our ears or a tingling on our skin. As our sensory perceptions expanded, we became more aware of our bodies responding to the vibration of the plants and the plants responding to us.

We began journeying with the drum and singing bowl as part of our meditation practice.

JOURNEY WITH THE DRUM
~ Judith ~

CHEROKEE ELDER WILL ROCKINGBEAR lived in the mountains of North Carolina and I am grateful to him for being my teacher and sharing his wisdom. He taught his students how to journey with a frame drum using a particular drum beat. Rockingbear called it dreaming with the drum. This dream journey enables one to travel to invisible worlds, beyond ordinary reality. One of his favorite teachings was pay attention, and he would say this three times.

To dream with the drum, one person plays the drum, staying engaged with the process. The person that is journeying, sits or lies down with their eyes closed; travelling on the sound waves. The drum beat has to be a moderately fast rhythmic beat, about four to five beats per second. This rhythm enables the dreamer to journey to the dreamtime. The drummer plays for ten to fifteen minutes and then plays a call back beat alerting the dreamer to come back to the present moment. There are many reasons why you would want to journey, as it expands your perceptions. You may want to ask a question, meet a plant spirit or get support for healing.

One day I drummed for Paulette while she journeyed. On the journey she met a plant spirit. She described seeing yellowish-green light and out of the light, a caterpillar-like being with green wings emerged that communicated to her in images. This was an extraordinary moment in our work with plants. Paulette felt a new doorway of perception had opened for her.

JOURNEY WITH THE SINGING BOWL

CONNECTING TO THE VIBRATION OF SOUND supports the clearing, opening, and balancing of your energy body. The water and blood in our body conducts the sound waves to all the cells.

We played a singing bowl, feeling the sound vibrations move through us, the garden, and the land. We would gently strike the side of the bowl with a rubber mallet, as it is easier to get a consistent rhythm. Every singing bowl is unique, so you might want to search for the bowl that feels best for you.

You can set an intention for the healing sounds to assist you. If you work with spirit guides and helpers you can also call on them to guide you in your journey.

Play your bowl in front of your heart and or solar plexus area to help with opening your energy body. This will assist you in clearing out any blocked energy so you can be more receptive. Allow the vibrations of the sound to flow around and through you. You can repeat this several times until you feel more clear, open and balanced.

When you feel ready to connect with a plant, consider playing the bowl softly, so as not to overwhelm the plant's energy. Begin by

speaking loving intentions towards the plant. You could ask the plant a question. An example could be, "What teaching can you share with me today?" We like to speak out loud when communicating with nature. When speaking out loud we are acknowledging the plant and also adding a vibratory imprint to the conversation.

Close your eyes and gently play the bowl for ten to fifteen minutes. Let the sound waves carry you on a journey to the plant, using your expanded awareness to enter the dreamtime.

If the practice of journeying is new to you, you can ask a friend to try this practice with you. One person can play the singing bowl while the other person journeys and then you can switch roles. As with drumming, use a call back beat to help the person return from their dreaming.

You may want to journal any images you receive. As with waking up from a dream, you may find that the images and messages can quickly fade.

We resonated with the singing bowl in the key of E, which is associated with the third chakra or solar plexus area. Paulette played the singing bowl, while I journeyed to a plant. In these journeys I received messages and felt more connected to the plant's medicine.

CHANTING

Most ceremonies in cultures all over the world use singing and chanting…because chanting in ceremony creates a pathway for beauty and awareness …it affects our bodies on a cellular level and it affects all the Earth and plants as well. It frees stuck energy in us and in the world around us. ~ JOSEPH RAEL

GRANDFATHER JOSEPH TAUGHT US THAT CHANTING is a way to bring our attention to the present moment so we can listen more deeply. We have been given permission to share his teachings on chanting, and we offer it so that you can bring this practice into your relationship with the plants.

We can connect with what Grandfather calls the "principal vibrations of creation" by chanting the vowel sounds. As a native Tiwa and Spanish speaker, he uses the Spanish pronunciation of the vowel sounds as a basis for this teaching:

If possible sit near the plant or imagine the plant in front of you as you chant.

Bring your full attention to a plant by chanting or singing its name.

Borage would be Boor-ahhg, Boor-ahhg, Boor-ahhg.

When you are comfortable chanting the plant's name, then try chanting just the vowel sounds of its name like "oh" or "ah" in borage.

Chant Oh-ah, Oh-ah, Oh-ah, and feel the vibration resonating in your body.

These two vowel sounds of "oh" and "ah" bring the energies of innocence and awareness into your chanting practice.

After you are done chanting, pay attention to the silence that follows.

The silence holds creative potential.

You may have to practice chanting for a while to become comfortable using your voice.

TEACHINGS ON THE SPANISH VOWEL SOUNDS FROM JOSEPH RAEL

A   (Ahh) = Purification

The sound of "Ahh" is about physical cleansing as well as spiritual cleansing.

E   (Eh) = Relationship

The sound of "Eh" is about your relationship with all the people and beings in your life, the invisible as well as the visible.

I   (Eee) = Awareness

The sound of "Eee" is about the place where insight comes into consciousness.

O   (Oh) = Innocence

The sound of "Oh" means child-like innocence. Open to the process of evolving, unfolding, growing with the essence of curiosity.

U   (Uu) = Carrying

The sound of "Uu" is carrying us to the heart center of the Great Mystery. In whatever work we are doing we can tap into the transformational potential of highest awareness.

Your body is like a vibratory instrument. Group chanting magnifies the effect because the whole body is feeling the vibration of many voices pinging upon it. ~ JOSEPH RAEL

CHANTING THE DIRECTIONS OF THE MEDICINE WHEEL

WHEN WE FIRST BEGAN TO CHANT in Paulette's medicine wheel garden, it helped us to open to the intelligence of Nature by aligning with the four directions. We first lit some incense to cleanse our spiritual body. Then we faced the four directions, starting in the East, moving to the South, the West and the North. We chanted the vowel sounds for each direction turning at last to the center, the place of transformational potential.

When we were finished with our chanting, we closed the directions by chanting in each direction again, expressing our appreciation for the sacred space and support we received.

PLANTING THE GARDEN

CHANT AS YOU PLANT SEEDS, VISUALIZING THE POTENTIAL each seed has to unfold. Chant "eee" for the word seed and also because the "eee" sound carries the vibration of awareness. By chanting with love and awareness, you are creating a planting ceremony.

We generally use heirloom seeds because they help to preserve the genetic diversity of the planet. If you let some of the plants go to seed in the fall, you can save the seeds to plant the following spring.

Watching the plants emerge from the soil is watching the miracle of life unfold. Some of the seeds will germinate and thrive and become food and medicine. When the seedlings come up in the garden, we sing or chant to them. They are in a tender stage in their development, and we want to encourage their growth.

If you purchase plants, gently remove them from their container and handle their roots carefully. Dig a hole that is wide enough so that the newly liberated roots can take hold in the earth. This too can be done as a planting ceremony, chanting the name of the plant. We hope you explore chanting in your own garden and invite your friends to join you.

PLANT INTELLIGENCE

RESEARCH HAS SHOWN THAT PLANTS PERCEIVE their environment, have memory, exist in a social network, and signal to each other. There is a species of evening primrose, Oenothera drummondii, that responds to the beating of bee wings by producing a sweeter nectar in order to attract the bees. There is a higher concentration of sugar when the bee's wings are vibrating near the plant. Think of the flowers as the ears of the plant listening for pollinators such as the bees, butterflies, and birds. (Donahue)

If we consider the ability to adapt and survive over time, plants have been on the planet longer than humans by hundreds of millions of years. One of their survival strategies is incredible diversity. An example is Verbascum thapsus, known as common mullein, which is part of the figwort family with over 300 species. This diversity helps plants to adapt to environmental changes and protect themselves from diseases and predators.

While some plants can adapt, others are more vulnerable to the impact of human development and loss of habitat. On the United Plant Savers website is a current list of plants that are at risk in the United States and Canada. (See resources). People aware of endangered plants will often dig up and relocate plants to safer locations when there is habitat disruption.

Plants are going extinct at a rate 500 times faster than before human development. "Since botanist Carl Linnaeus published Species Plantarum, a compendium of every known plant until 1753, at least 571 species of seed-bearing plants have gone extinct around the world." ("Nearly 600 Plant Species Have Gone Extinct In Last 250 Years").

Plants are able to signal warnings and support to others in their
plant community. For example, zoologists from Pretoria University
document a case of acacia trees protecting themselves from herds
of antelope by producing lethal quantities of tannin. The first trees
being nibbled by the antelope were destroyed, then trees nearby
started upping their production of leaf tannin and released a chemical,
ethylene, into the air signalling other trees in the grove to up their
own production of tannin. The result was the antelope ate the lethal
doses of tannin and died, but the grove of acacia trees survived
(Hughes).

Plants are the only beings on Earth that make their own
food directly from the energy of the sun, this process is called

photosynthesis. The chlorophyll molecule that makes photosynthesis possible in plants is chemically similar to the hemoglobin in our blood. This similarity shows our kinship to our green ancestors, but, alas, the only way we can make a green energy drink from the sun is to make it with plants.

Plants and trees provide us with the food to eat, air to breathe, and this beautiful green and blue planet to live on. Most of our early medicines were made from plants, and many of our modern allopathic medicines are also derived from plants.

RECIPROCITY IS DEFINED AS THE PRACTICE OF EXCHANGING something with others for mutual benefit. Plants and trees give us gifts of food, medicine, oxygen and beauty. What can we give in return?

Sometimes I feel guided to just give a plant my heartfelt gratitude. I talk to the plants when I go out to the garden, telling them how beautiful they are.

I might leave offerings of sea shells, cornmeal, or stones that I have found.

In offering reciprocity with plants, you can start by being aware of the plant's needs. Plants need water to survive and you can offer them the blessing of water. Sometimes I offer reciprocity by tending to the plant, trimming back dead leaves, mulching, and gently touching its leaves. Appreciation of the plant's beauty and medicine are part of reciprocity.

If you don't have a backyard or garden space, maybe you have a friend who would welcome you to be in their garden. If you live in a city there are botanical gardens or parks you can visit where you can be with plants. You can easily grow some herbs in pots like thyme, calendula, or basil. You can have a houseplant that you care for and practice reciprocity with.

I created an altar next to the garden as a place to leave offerings for the nature spirits of the land. On this altar are crystals, stones, shells, beads, and a bell I sometimes ring before meditation. In the summer I place a bowl of water on the altar and add flowers from the garden, creating a gift of beauty and welcoming.

FORGIVENESS CEREMONY

WHILE WE EXIST ON THIS BEAUTIFUL PLANET, harm to nature and other species is inevitable, even if we do our best to tread lightly on the earth. Forgiving ourselves for the harm we have done to others and nature is life-changing work.

Creating and participating in a forgiveness ceremony has helped me enter into a deeper relationship with the garden and nature.

- Find a quiet space outside in nature. If for any reason you can not go outside, inside will work too. It is your intention that matters. Turn off any electronic devices so you won't be interrupted.

- Prepare yourself by grounding and centering yourself.

- Play a drum, rattle, flute or singing bowl. Sing a song or chant before you begin. You may want to light some incense, or have a candle with you. Bring whatever tools help you to enter a sacred space.

- Connect to the ancestors of the land by acknowledging their presence. You are showing respect to those who have come before. For example, I acknowledge the Sissipahaw Indians who once lived in this area.

- Here are suggestions for a forgiveness ceremony. You can write your own if you prefer.

I humbly ask for forgiveness from Nature and Mother Earth— the plants, trees, birds, animals, fish, insects, the earth below and sky above—for any harm or injury I may have caused them in this lifetime.

I forgive myself for any harm I have caused.

I allow unconditional love and compassion to be present in this moment.

I express gratitude for the earth and all beings that are present, seen and unseen.

I send you my love, I send you my gratitude, and I acknowledge you.

Sit quietly and pay attention to feelings that arise in your body.

JUDITH BROOKS

Grounding and
One with All Meditation

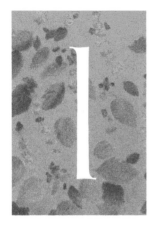I am an intuitive healer and Judith asked me if I would share some teachings about meditation and help bring forward some of the messages from the plants. It has been an honor and a privilege to sit with the plants and help these beautiful plant teachers to come into your life.

In my late twenties, I was working with a healer and we were journeying together through a past life regression. She described a cabin, near a river, with plants hanging and drying on the porch. She reflected from her vision that I was a skilled herbalist in the mountains of North Carolina. When I came out of that journey, my healing practitioner laid a map down on her desk and asked me to show her where the cabin was located. I scanned my hand over the map and pointed to a place near Burnsville, NC. In this lifetime, I had visited that land many times, and continue to visit there.

Perhaps we don't lose the stories in our past lifetimes; we only add to them and bring the gifts forward. In this lifetime, I don't live in a cabin in the woods, but I do continue my relationship with plants.

My father is a funeral director in a funeral home that has been in his family line for 250 years. My mother is a horticulturist and a musician who can grow anything and soothe anyone. Somewhere between death and blooming, I learned a lot about dying, living, and a deep respect for all living beings.

At a young age, I was often teased by other children. I found solace in the natural world. I would go down to the creek behind our house and talk with the plants and create little villages for all of the fairies. My mother started a rhododendron nursery, and I would spend time talking with the plants, celebrating the blooms, and tenderly caring for the other plants that I was so fortunate to share my childhood with.

Fast forward many years: I had found my way to tending the light of others through many forms of energy medicine and intuitive healing. As I found my roots in the area where I live, I too was called to the Sound Chamber and the teachings of Grandfather Joseph Rael. I dedicated many of my personal practices to his teachings and the honoring of the planet.

Amelia

GROUNDING IS A SIMPLE, YET PROFOUND, PRACTICE that clears and strengthens your energy system by intentionally connecting you to the essential energies of Mother Earth.

The effects and depth of your grounding practice depends entirely on your intention and focus going into the practice. The more that you cultivate a practice in which your intention is guided by your heart, not your mind, and where your focus is centered on harmony, not the process, the more your practice will deepen.

Sacred conversations between all living beings are complex and beautiful exchanges of energies and intentions. Before you enter into sacred conversation with the plants, it is important to ground yourself so that you can offer yourself to the conversation in a humble, loving, and respectful manner.

When coming to speak with the plants (or to any living being), you will want to enter into that conversation humbly, connected to a grateful heart, connected to Mother Earth, and connected to Greater Spirit.

When you are being humble, you offer an unfinished version of yourself to the conversation. This is also true when you are connecting with plants. Humbleness allows you to acknowledge that there are parts of you that are still growing and helps you to listen with an open mind and open heart. It implies a willingness to change and evolve as a human being.

You may use the following Grounding Meditation to support your conversations with the plants.

PREPARING FOR YOUR GROUNDING MEDITATION

TAKE A FEW MOMENTS TO CENTER before you arrive in the place of your meditation take the time to notice your surroundings and feel where the energy is calling you to be. You may wish to extend a few kind and loving words towards yourself.

When you sit outside, let the earth be a source of grounding for you. If you can, take off your shoes and feel the softness of the grass and the warmth of the soil. Feel roots extending out of your feet, going deeply into the earth supporting you. Bring your attention to your breath and breathe in the fresh air.

If there is something specific on your heart or mind, it can be beneficial to notice and name what you are feeling. You can then speak these words to the plants, the earth, or Source so you can be supported.

If you are feeling disconnected from Source, bring to mind the beauty of a full moon, a starlit sky, a flower, a tree, a sunset or sunrise. Being with the beauty of the natural world can bring you into a deeper alignment.

Speak or sing the name of your Higher Power once, and then let the echo of this name repeat itself in your being. This would be like striking a gong and allowing the echo to reverberate filling the space. You can repeat this as many times as you like.

Connect to the love you have for another individual, or an animal or plant, and feel that love deeply within your heart. As you connect to the vibration of love, know that you are also connecting to the vibration of Source.

PREPARATION FOR ONE WITH ALL MEDITATION

YOU CAN DO THIS MEDITATION INSIDE WITH THE INTENTION to connect to nature, but if it is possible to be outside with the trees, the plants, the stones, the flying ones, the crawling ones, the swimming ones, you will be with wonderful, supportive, and welcoming company.

What you will need:

🍃 A quiet place in nature or indoors that will be undisturbed.

🍃 A container of water.

Disconnect from all electronic devices. Find a comfortable place where you feel safe and at ease. When you feel ready to start your communication with the plants, you may want to use your breath to bring yourself into a deeper connection with the garden.

Take three deep, slow breaths and imagine that your breath is connected with the plant's respiration cycle.

Inhale the gift of oxygen from the trees and plants. Exhale that which no longer serves. Feel this as a prayerful offering.

Continue to breathe into the circulation of this breath of oneness with the plants. With each inhale, bring the earth ever deeper into your body. With each exhale, offer the earth ever deeper prayers of gratitude. Allow yourself a few moments to breathe in the celebration of this reunion.

The earth invites us to sit down and listen. This meditation can be used to connect with the plants to help support your conversation.

ONE WITH ALL MEDITATION

Request the energies of the Creator for guidance and protection.

Allow your heart to bloom in gratitude for this support.

Affirm the presence of your Higher Self.

Request the energies of your Highest Self so that you may bring your truth to this conversation.

Allow your heart to bloom in gratitude for this opportunity.

Affirm the presence of the plant that you wish to listen to and speak with.

Request the energies of this beautiful living being.

Allow your heart to bloom in gratitude for the invitation.

Affirm the peaceful joining with this plant in communion.

Sit for a few moments within the space of your connection to Source, to your Higher Self, and with the plant whom you wish to listen to and speak with.

Notice how this space around you feels as though it is held by a sacred container.

The space itself is rich with the energies of fertile conversation.

Feel yourself sitting on the Earth within this space of protection and inspiration.

Feel your body being held by the Earth below you.

Allow your heart to bloom in gratitude for being held.

Extend yourself by intention, growing your legs, as if they are roots.

Allow them to follow the energetic whisper from the soil of the Earth.

Allow your heart to bloom in gratitude for being seen and acknowledged.

Feel your roots deepening through the topsoil, deep into the layers of the Earth.

Experience the energies of this life-sustaining Earth rising into your roots.

Allow your heart to bloom in gratitude for being nurtured.

Notice how the energies of the earth flow up through your roots and into your body.

These energies follow the lines of energy that flow like rivers through you.

Allow your heart to bloom in the presence of this energetic reunion.

Feel how these energies effortlessly follow the rivers to your heart and flow endlessly into your center.

Allow your heart to bloom in gratitude for this infinite river of loving energy.

Feel your connection to All Beings through the songs of nature around you.

Experience the voices singing together in One song. Allow your heart to bloom in gratitude for the opportunity to listen.

Know that as you sit fully supported, you are singing the remembered One song.

Your greatest gift in this moment is to offer your presence and listen openly for any messages from the plant. Give yourself time to sit in this grounded and supported place in quiet meditation.

CLOSING THE MEDITATION

After your meditation with the plant, you may end with any combination of the following steps:

- Express your gratitude to Mother Earth, and the plants for the opportunity to share this sacred space.
- Offer a blessing to the plant and offer some of the water you brought.
- Thank the plant beings for their support.

Slowly begin to bring movement to your body and return yourself to an everyday awareness.

Get up slowly and walk until you have a strong and clear connection with your physical body.

Meditation with plants is a little like learning to hear music. Some of us are born with perfect pitch, but most have to develop a sense for sound. Like practicing the notes of a musical scale, meditation is something we can practice, developing a sense for the language of plants.

The Plants

O ver many seasons we meditated in our gardens and developed a deeper sense of trust and connection with the plants. We created ceremonies, chanted, meditated and journeyed. In quiet moments we received images and healing messages from the plants.

The ten plants in this chapter are the ones with whom we developed a close relationship. We introduce each plant with an essay on its historical, cultural and present day usage, followed by a message received during our meditations. Our friend Amelia is an intuitive healer who conveys these messages in her eloquent prose.

Dodi O'Neill, our friend, painted each of these plants from her garden in California. Her beautiful paintings bring the glowing qualities of the plants to light. The photos were taken of plants in both Paulette's and Judith's gardens in North Carolina.

GLOSSARY OF HERBAL PROPERTIES AND ACTIONS

THESE HERBAL TERMS ARE COMMONLY USED TO DESCRIBE the healing properties and functions of herbs. This short introduction will help you to build an herbal vocabulary, as you continue to study and be with the plants. Some herbs have many therapeutic actions and will belong to more than one category. We are using examples of the herbs used in this book, many more herbs can be added to each category.

Adaptogens are herbs that aid in supporting the body's ability to adapt to stress. These herbs can help support the body's endocrine, immune, and nervous systems. Holy Basil is an example of an adaptogen.

Alteratives are herbs that aid in elimination of wastes in the body through the blood, lymphatic, bowels, and skin. These herbs support detoxification of the body. Calendula, rosemary and elder flowers are examples of alterative herbs.

Antispasmodic are herbs that help relax muscles and relieve muscle spasms and cramps in the body. Blue vervain is one example.

Antivirals are herbs that help support the immune system to fight off viruses. Elderberry and thyme are examples of antiviral herbs.

Astringents herbs help in tightening, toning and strengthening tissues in the mucous membranes and blood vessels. Some of these herbs can help form a protective layer over injured skin. Mullen and plaintain are examples of mild astringents.

Nervines are herbs that support and strengthen the nervous system. They can help reduce stress, anxiety and nervousness. Blue vervain and holy basil are examples of a nervine.

Vulnerary are herbs that can be applied externally to the skin to help heal, repair and treat skin infections. They are sometimes used in poultices. Calendula, plantain and thyme are examples.

LATIN:
Verbena hastata

FAMILY:
Verbenaceae

COMMON:
Holy Herb,
Enchanter's Plant

Blue Vervain

One touch of nature makes the whole world kin.

WILLIAM SHAKESPEARE
playwright and poet (1564–1616)

BLUE VERVAIN IS A PERENNIAL PLANT WITH SMALL, five-petaled flowers, ranging from lilac to purple, with serrated leaves. The tall, slender spikes can grow from three to four feet tall and prefer wet meadows or moist, well-drained soil and a sunny location.

Blue Vervain is native to the United States and was used by American Indians to treat coughs, colds, and fevers. The European Vervain, *Verbena Officinalis,* was used in rituals by the Druids and known as the Enchanter's Plant. The Druids would harvest vervain at the dark of the moon and leave an offering of honeycomb on the earth in exchange.

Blue vervain has a bitter flavor and can be used as a tea to improve digestion. It is great for helping with neck tension and for muscle spasms. Blue vervain's calming properties help with anxiety and nervous tension, as it is a nervine, which means it is part of a category of herbs that strengthens the nervous system. This herb helps to promote menstruation and relieve cramps and pain. It is a cooling plant and can help with premenstrual stress and hot flashes for menopausal women.

SAFETY CONSIDERATIONS: *Not recommended for use during pregnancy.*

MEDITATION

IT'S AUGUST AND BLUE VERVAIN'S BEAUTIFUL SPIRAL FLOWERS are like a plethora of wizards' caps. We collect the flowering tops and leaves for tea and remember to leave some flowers for the bees.

Blue vervain's voice has an interesting vibration—a high-pitched sound, like an electric hum. It is relaxing, resembling the community buzzing of many bees.

My gift for you is a message of comfort. You can use the sound of the hum in my voice to help you clear that which is not serving you. Meditate with me and let my vibration come through your body. Hum with me so together we can create harmony and healing.

In my flowers, you will see the spiral design of healing.

On each spiral step of your healing is one of my flowers.

Each time you take another step on your journey, another flower opens as a gift to you.

When you look at me you can remember how far you have come along your healing path.

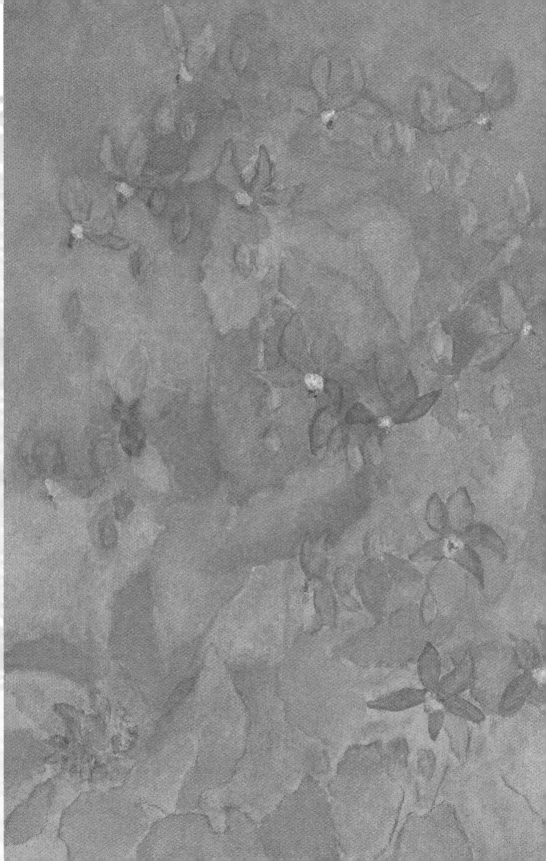

LATIN:
Borago officinalis
FAMILY:
Boraginaceae
COMMON:
Star Flower, Bee Plant

Borage

Let Nature be your teacher.

WILLIAM WORDSWORTH
poet (1770–1850)

BORAGE GROWS THROUGHOUT EUROPE AND NORTH AMERICA
and is an annual plant that self-seeds easily in the garden. The
beautiful star-shaped blue flowers are rich in nectar and attract many
bees to the garden, hence the name "Bee Plant." Borage flowers have
prominent black pointy centers known as anthers, where the pollen
of the flower is released.

The leaves and stems have coarse hairs and a cucumber-like
fragrance. In Europe borage leaves are used as a culinary herb in
soups and the flowers added to herbal teas, or candied. I like to plant
borage in my vegetable garden as a "companion plant" for tomatoes
and cabbages because it is said to help reduce the numbers of tomato
hornworms and cabbage worms in the garden.

Borage has been used in European herbalism for centuries and
is especially known to dispel melancholy, help restore the adrenals
for people who are exhausted and to treat coughs and sore throats.
In the United States the leaves of this herb are not recommended
for internal use because of the alkaloids contained in them, but the

flowers are edible. The seeds of borage are a rich source of gamma-linolenic acid (GLA), and used to make borage seed oil. This oil is used for skin conditions such as eczema and dry skin.

John Gerard, an herbalist from the 17th century translated a Roman saying, "*Ego borago gaudiansemper ago. I borage always bring courage.*" This saying was said to be recited by Roman soldiers before going into battle.

SAFETY CONSIDERATIONS: Borage leaves contain low amounts of pyrrolizidine alkaloids also known as "PA's," which can be toxic to the liver. Not recommended for internal use.

MEDITATION

I ASK THE BORAGE PLANT FOR PERMISSION TO EAT A FLOWER and sit in meditation.

The sun warms the back of my heart. My chakra centers are like flower blossoms, opening. I can hear her speaking both from the center of her flower and also the pointed ends of her flower petals. The sound it creates is an echo.

Come, she says.

Come, as the echo, the whisper, after . . .

Do not be fooled by my daintiness and my softness.

Do not be fooled by my daintiness and my softness.

Do not get too comfortable with yourself in my presence.

Do not get too comfortable with yourself in my presence.

Allow yourself to be light.

Allow yourself to be light.

Do you see the deep tunnel in the center of my flower?

Do you see the deep tunnel in the center of my flower?

Together we will travel the time folds of the universe.

Together we will travel the time folds of the universe.

This is the doorway beyond places, spaces, and time.

This is the doorway beyond places, spaces, and time.

This is the portal between generations.

This is the portal between generations

I will open the doorways to the yet unborn.

I will open the doorways to the yet unborn.

Through me you can sit in conversation and learn your pure potential.

Through me you can sit in conversation and learn your pure potential.

I will teach you to bring this perspective to your life

And I will teach you to bring this perspective to your life

And you will meet life with courage; you will be unafraid.

And you will meet life with courage; you will be unafraid.

There is a portal in the center of her flower that opens when we are in her presence. There is an invitation to join her there, like sitting at the entrance of the Universal Womb.

LATIN:
Calendula officinalis
FAMILY:
Asteraceae
COMMON:
Pot Marigold

Calendula

An "herb of the sun" with much of the sun's power in its flowers.

JULIETTE DE BAIRACLI LEVY
herbalist and author (1912–2009)

CALENDULA IS A BEAUTIFUL ANNUAL THAT ORIGINATED in North Africa and later migrated to Europe, the Americas and Asia. This plant is associated with the divine feminine and one of its names is "Marygold" because it bloomed during festivals honoring the Mother Mary. Another name, "Tara's flower," is named for Tara, the Tibetan Goddess of Compassion. Calendula is not to be confused with the common Marigold, *Tagetes erecta*, which is native to the Americas.

The aromatic flower heads and their sticky green bases contain the plant's medicinal properties and are dried to make tea or infused into an oil for body care and healing of the skin. Harvest calendula flowers on dry sunny days, when the flowers are fully open. Calendula flowers are associated with the sun and its crescent shaped seeds with the moon. There are many varieties of calendula with colors ranging from orange, golden yellow to reddish-brown, like the shades of a beautiful sunrise.

Calendula is known as a soothing balm for the skin and used externally in salves and compresses for treating burns, skin abrasions, eczema, and dry, itchy skin. It can sooth mild sunburn as it cools the heat of the burn. It also has antiseptic properties, so it helps to limit bacterial growth on the skin.

Calendula tea can help settle an upset stomach, ease a sore throat, or can be used as a compress for insect stings or wound healing. Fresh calendula petals are edible and high in antioxidants and can be added to salads.

SAFETY CONSIDERATIONS: If you are allergic to chamomile or ragweed this herb may cause a rare reaction so proceed with caution. Not recommended for internal use during pregnancy,

MEDITATION

I ENTER THE GARDEN AS DAWN IS BREAKING. The golden calendula flowers are covered with dew. Soon the dew will dry, the petals will open and I will collect the flowers for medicine.

Calendula's rays of petals are yellow like the rays of the sun and the color of the third chakra. Chanting the vowel sounds of calendula, I feel warmth in my solar plexus.

After connecting with her, there was no invitation to "come" or "sit" to listen. Sometimes the natural world will speak to you in images beyond words. I call this visual listening.

I first flew outside of my body so that I could see the entire planet from space. It reminded me of the beautiful pictures from the space station where the planet is visible in a misty blue, and the oceans, clouds, and continents appear below. The image also included the stars and the farthest galaxies painted in the dark sky beyond our beautiful blue planet.

As I focused, I became aware of Mother Earth's heartbeat. From this heartbeat the energy of calendula was pulsing, curling ribbons of golden, misty energy throughout the planet~in the land, in the seas, in the air.

The sensation that I felt was one of a great heart opening. It was as if my own heartbeat like calendula was beginning to ribbon that same golden misty energy throughout my entire body. I felt an overwhelming sense of divine compassion and oneness with our beautiful planet, Mother Earth.

Visual Listening

It is important to remember that when you listen to the natural world, sometimes the natural world will speak to you beyond words. This is true of working with energy in people or animals, too. Visual listening is connected to a specific part of your energy system, called the third eye or brow chakra. This part of your energy system allows you to see information through still images or movies. I am referring to it here as visual listening because sitting with the plants allows us to open into the conversation and receive their messages through the visual. More traditionally, this might be called expanded sight, higher sight, visual empathy, or clairvoyance.

LATIN:
(American Elderberry)
Sambucus canadensis

FAMILY:
Adoxaceae

COMMON:
Elder Mother,
Lady Elder

Elderberry

The earth laughs in flowers.

RALPH WALDO EMERSON
American poet, essayist (1803–1882)

ELDER IS REFERRED TO AS "NATURE'S MEDICINE CHEST"
because most of the plant has been used medicinally through the ages.
The large, beautiful, lacey flowers can be used fresh or dried. Drinking
a warm cup of elderflower tea can stimulate sweating and help reduce
a fever, as the flowers are very cooling to the body.

Elderberry is known for modulating the immune system and
there are many studies showing it helps reduce the duration of flus
and colds. The dark purple berries have anthocyanins, which is a
nutrient that helps protect blood vessel walls, reduce inflammation,
and promote heart health. Elderberries have more antioxidants than
blueberries and are rich in minerals too.

The ripe purple berries are cooked and mashed through a fine
mesh sieve. The seeds are discarded and the delicious purple juice is
made into a syrup with honey.

Historically, the European variety of elder was associated with a mythical wise woman called Lady Elder who lived in the elder bush. The plant was highly respected and offerings were left for elder before harvesting its medicine. Leaves of elder were hung outside the door to protect the house from evil.

It is June and the cream-colored flowers are in bloom. By July the flowers will have turned into purple berries. Nearing the elder bush with our baskets, we can smell the fragrant blossoms and watch the bees busily gathering pollen. The flowers are ready to be harvested for the elderflower cordial that we are going to make today. After we lay our elderflowers on a towel, many tiny insects make their way out of the blossoms. We gently carry the insects back outside.

We use just the flowers for the cordial and not the green stems. We place the flowers in a bowl and prepare a simple syrup of sugar and water, heating it until the sugar dissolves. When the syrup is still hot, we pour the liquid over the flowers, letting them steep for about six hours. We strain the flowers out and the remaining liquid is a delicious cordial which has a remarkable floral flavor.

SAFETY CONSIDERATIONS: Do not eat raw elderberries as this can cause severe digestive distress such as nausea, diarrhea and vomiting. Only use ripe berries and always cook them before consuming and strain the seeds out. Elderberry has not been proven to be safe for use during pregnancy.

MEDITATION

I ASK PERMISSION OF THE ELDER AND CUT A DEAD STALK from the bush. The stalks of the elderberry can be turned into a flute-like instrument.

I blow through the stem and imagine Pan, the half-goat, half-man nature spirit, playing music in my garden with an elder flute. I chant through the hollow stalk, and listen for a message from Mother Elder.

I feel as though she winked at me, sort of like a grandmother who

shares a teaching that is so big there is nothing left to do but to smile. She adds some humor so as to soften the direct teaching and yet not diminish its power.

"*Sit,*" she said, and paused. "*Do not talk. Just be quiet.*"

Her voice was commanding and yet all-loving and kind.

She is the Elder Mother. She loves unconditionally.

"*Live from your honesty, your purity, your integrity. Do not pretend to be what you are not. Just be who you are and you will heal the world.*"

I asked her if she wanted to share anything else, to which she replied, "*What else is there to share?*" and smiled at me.

After meditating with elderberry, I saw her in a vision. The Spirit of Elderberry seemed to come from a sunset in the West, the tender place where the day breaks into starlight. She was calling the stars to aid in the navigation of those who are journeying.

After this vision, I was left with the image of her flowers open, like lacy constellations against the backdrop of the garden.

It was early Spring and Judith brought me an elder start. It was a stick with a few roots beginning to sprout. She had read it was easy to get an elder started by cutting healthy stems from a mature bush and leaving the cut ends in a bucket of water for a few weeks. "I don't know if it will grow," she said.

"My mother told me that anything would grow beneath this window. It gets the morning sun." We dug up the earth, put the stick in the ground, and added a little water.

Elder Mother was a plant my Celtic ancestors planted in their gardens because it helped with many ailments, in addition to making delicious jelly.

The start Judith brought took root and over the next few years outgrew its little plot beneath the window. We were able to take some cuttings from this bush and start another elder in the backyard. We have enjoyed its floral beauty and plethora of purple berries for many years.

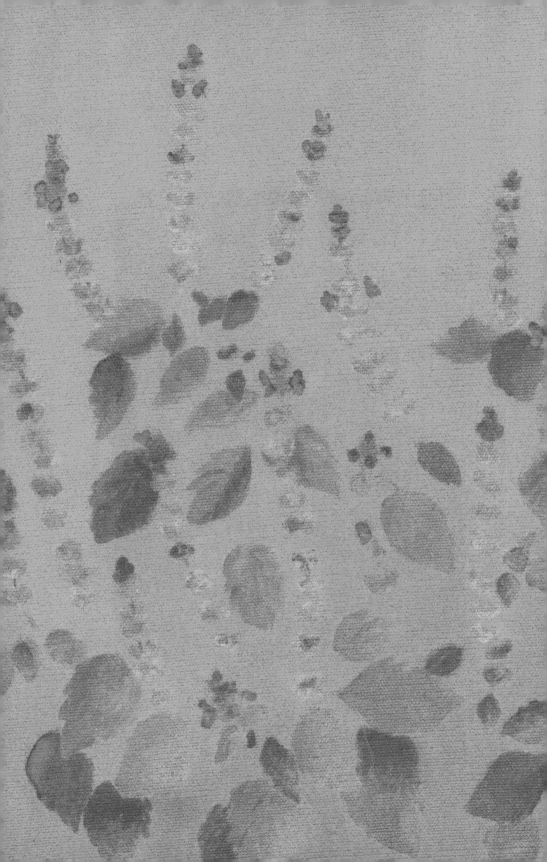

LATIN:
Tulsi Krishna,
Ocimum tenuiflorum,
Tulsi Vana,
O. gratissimum,
Tulsi Kapoor, O. sanctum

FAMILY:
Lamiaceae

COMMON:
Sacred Basil, Tulsi

Holy Basil

The Incomparable One.

AYURVEDIC TEXT
1,000 AD

THIS VENERABLE PLANT IS AN IMPORTANT HERB in Ayurvedic medicine and is native to India, Pakistan, Thailand, and Malaysia. Tulsi is revered in Hinduism and is considered the plant manifestation of the feminine goddess, Lakshmi, the consort to the Hindu god, Lord Vishnu. She is grown in dedicated spaces in temples and thought to aid with meditation.

I first learned about holy basil at an herb conference in North Carolina and purchased a few different varieties and planted them in a sunny place in the garden. They thrived in the heat of a North Carolina summer.

Over the years I dried the plant's leaves for tea, made tinctures, and holy basil oil. I sang her praises to my friends and encouraged them to try a cup of tea. Many people have spoken about its abilities to help with mental stress and brain fog. Tulsi helps with cerebral circulation, blood sugar imbalances and supports the body's ability to adapt to stress.

The plants are easy to grow in warm climates. After I established a few plants, there has been an abundance of tulsi year after year. At summer's end, I leave a few plants in the garden to go to seed. The tulsi seeds scatter themselves through my garden. In the spring the tiny plants emerge when the soil is warm. When they bloom the beautiful purple blossoms attract bees to the garden. Tulsi tastes unique as it is pungent, warm and sweet. The scents of pepper, anise, citrus, cinnamon, and clove can be found in the different varieties.

SAFETY CONSIDERATIONS: Not recommended for use during pregnancy.

MEDITATION

IN THE EARLY MORNING LIGHT, HOLY BASIL GLISTENS with dew. It is nature's blessing of liquid light. I place a leaf on my tongue and close my eyes. A burst of light in the shape of a star radiates in four directions. I taste her pungent leaves and know we are connected. My tongue continues to tingle as the burst of light grows.

I am a body of light imprinted with the holy light of holy basil. Not saved from the physical, which has its cycle of living and dying, but transformed.

I hear the notes of her many songs sung in harmony.

When I feel sadness, I can hear the song of joy offering itself to me in my sadness.

When I feel anxious, I can feel the song of calm offering itself to me in my anxiety.

When I feel worn out, I can hear the song of rejuvenation offering itself to the worn out parts of me.

This is what I mean by many songs. It feels as though whatever I bring to the conversation, she can offer the medicine to meet that need.

LATIN:
Verbascum thapsus

FAMILY:
Scrophulariaceae

COMMON:
*Candlewick plant,
Lungwort, Blanket herb*

Mullein

The plants have enough spirit to transform our limited vision.

ROSEMARY GLADSTAR
herbalist and author (1948–)

THERE ARE OVER 300 SPECIES OF MULLEIN WITH FLOWERS
ranging from yellow, light pink, to white. Mullein is a tenacious plant
that grows in abandoned fields, alongside the highways, and even out
of the cracks of sidewalks. Mullein is a biennial herb which means
it has a two-year life cycle. The first year the woolly leaves form a
rosette pattern. The second year it produces a tall flower spike and
then dies, but is reborn with its seeds.

Mullein has many strategies for sowing its seed and a plant may
mysteriously show up in your garden. You might find small mullein
plants in the spring near the dead stalks of last year's plants. To reseed
mullein, in the fall gather some of the tiny seeds from the mullein's
spike and sprinkle them around the borders and edges of your garden
where you would like more plants.

I like to touch the soft, woolly leaves of mullein and roll them in
my fingers. I see the connection between the softness of the leaves
and the soothing effects it has on the lungs. The dried leaves can be

smoked to ease a wheezing cough or asthma or added with other soothing herbs to a smoke mix. Mullein's leaves and roots can act like an expectorant, loosening up phlegm so it can be expelled from the lungs and throat.

Mullein leaf and flower tincture taken internally can gently help the body's lymphatic circulation. The lymphatic system is part of the immune system that helps with the removal of toxins and wastes from the body. A mullein poultice can help ease swollen lymph nodes. An oil made with organic olive oil and the fresh flowers of mullein can be gently dropped into the ear to soothe earaches.

Dried mullein spikes can be up to six feet tall. Historically they were dipped in tallow and were used as torches and known as Hag's Tapers. Candlewick is another name for mullein as dried mullein stems were made into lamp wicks.

MEDITATION

ON THE OUTSKIRTS OF PAULETTE'S CIRCULAR GARDEN, the tall, beautiful spike of mullein covered with tiny yellow flowers stands with sturdy strength.

We sit in silence, listening and communing with this beautiful vibrant plant asking permission to make a flower essence. We feel a "yes." Often this confirmation is felt as warmth in the solar plexus or around the heart. We begin to sing as we pluck the tiny flowers and place them in a small bowl of water in the sun. When the flower essence is complete we take a few drops and receive this message from mullein.

When used as a hag's taper we illuminate your path.

Taken as medicine we open the breath.

On my smoke your prayers are carried to the ancestors.

Remember your own light within.

LATIN:
(Broad leaf)
Plantago major
(Narrow leaf)
Plantago lanceolata
FAMILY:
Plantaginaceae
COMMON:
Ribwort plantain

Plantain

What is a weed?
A plant whose virtues have not yet been discovered.

RALPH WALDO EMERSON
American poet, essayist (1803–1882)

PLANTAIN IS NATIVE TO EUROPE. AMERICAN INDIANS called it White Man's Foot because the seeds were carried throughout North America on the soles of the settlers' shoes. Plantain grows in a rosette pattern and has strong parallel veins like ribs that go from the base to the tip of the leaf. You can find it growing in meadows, lawns, gardens and cracks in driveways and sidewalks.

This humble and common plant is an important medicinal herb. Due to its cooling properties, leaves of the narrow or broad leaf plantain can be made into a poultice for insect bites, splinters, poison ivy, stinging nettle stings, wounds and other inflamed skin conditions.

The leaves have antiseptic properties and contain allantoin which helps with skin tissue regeneration.

A poultice is an old, traditional method of healing. Crush a plant's leaves into a pulp with a blender or mortar and pestle. Apply the herbs directly to the skin. Wrap the area with gauze or a bandage to keep it in place. Change the poultice every 15–30 minutes as needed. If you are hiking in nature and get bitten or stung, you can crush and mash the leaves in your hands or with your teeth to create a poultice.

Many years ago I was in a park with a dear friend, Georgia Stone, who was in her early nineties. She got stung by a bee on her hand. She had developed a sensitivity to bee stings during her many years of farming and became anxious. I told Georgia about the healing properties of plantain, and she was willing to try it.

I noticed a patch of plantain at the edge of the woods where it hadn't been mowed. I asked permission of the plant to take a few of its leaves, and felt a confirmation in my heart that it was ok. I crushed and rolled a few leaves in my hands and placed the poultice on Georgia's hand. Gradually the swelling started going down and the pain eased.

She told me her "cure" for bee stings used to be a wet wad of chewing tobacco, but this plant, " . . . was working a whole lot better! God blessed me with the plantain cure today," she said.

Plantain works best when used fresh, especially for wounds, rashes and insect bites. Dried plantain leaves can be made into a tea for coughs and lung congestion. Add a little honey and sip to help ease hoarseness.

SAFETY CONSIDERATIONS: Plantain is considered a safe herb for children, the elderly and during pregnancy. If you get serious reactions to bee stings please seek medical assistance.

MEDITATION

IT IS AN EARLY MORNING IN LATE JULY and I sit in my garden meditating. I enjoy watching the droplets of rainbow-colored dew sparkle on the plants. I know the dew helps the plants prepare for the hot summer day that is in the forecast. Sitting down next to the plantain, I notice its flowering stalks have bits of pollen. I sing to plantain and then listen to the silence.

Sit with me and connect, she says, and beckons.

I welcome you to hear the voice within my many small flowers.
Listen widely, for you may hear my messages warbling.
These are my leaves singing a healing song.

Healer of simple wounds.
I hide my soothing gifts in a shroud of the everyday.
I welcome you to look deeper
into the ordinary.

I offer you my healing songs, disguised in a simple balm.

LATIN:
Salvia rosmarinus

FAMILY:
Lamiaceae

COMMON:
Dew of the Sea

Rosemary

There's rosemary, that's for remembrance; pray, love, remember …
WILLIAM SHAKESPEARE
playwright, poet (1564–1616)

NATIVE TO THE MEDITERRANEAN, ROSEMARY IS a perennial herb
that is grown worldwide. It is an evergreen herb that likes a sunny
spot in the garden and well-drained sandy soil. In very cold climates,
rosemary is grown in containers and brought inside during the winter.
In warm climates, the plants can grow into tall shrubs, and can flower
in the spring, fall, and into the early days of winter. Rosemary likes to
be on the dry side, so don't overwater this plant.

Rosemary is not just a culinary herb. It makes a tasty tea and is
known for improving cognition and memory, as it increases blood
circulation to the brain. There are chemical compounds in rosemary
that are being studied as a potential aid in slowing down deterioration
of the brain and the onset of cognitive issues.

Fresh or dried rosemary leaves added to epsom salts in baths are
helpful for muscle aches. The tea can also help with digestion.

SAFETY CONSIDERATIONS: Avoid applying rosemary essential oil on the skin during pregnancy. Rosemary is safe as a culinary herb in food during pregnancy. May be considered unsafe if used in medicinal amounts during pregnancy.

MEDITATION

I SIT WITH ROSEMARY AND WATCH HER beautiful periwinkle flowers glowing in the sunlight. As I reach out to touch the delicate flower, I feel an invitation to taste it.

The flower is like sweet nectar and I close my eyes and enter into a daydream. I am a young girl sitting in a garden near the sea. I can hear the ocean waves and taste the salty air. My brown dress is long and my dusty bare feet peek out. The bees are out collecting pollen from the tall rosemary plants on either side of me. I feel at peace in this place. The bees hum and I remember I am here to gather some rosemary for my mother, not to take a nap in the sun. The dream-like vision fades.

The rosemary in my garden has wintered over for several years and has grown to the size of a shrub. I got the start for this plant from the garden of an old friend. The rosemary in her yard, protected by the foundation of her two hundred year-old house, had survived many freezes and droughts. I remember digging deep around her plant to get a root, but still I was afraid my start would be traumatized by being torn from its longtime home. When I planted the root into the new soil of my garden, it shriveled and turned brown and lost its spiky aromatic leaves. I watered the plant and fertilized it, but it still didn't seem to take hold. It was brown and lifeless all that summer.

The next spring when I pushed the mulch back from the perennials, my heart leaped. There, looking young and healthy, was rosemary. She had not died at all but had been preparing herself for a strong rebirth with deep, hardy roots.

Rosemary grew in Jerusalem during the time of Christ, and some biblical stories say it was one of the herbs brought by the women who planned to prepare the body of the crucified Christ.

My own rosemary appeared to have died only to be reborn a healthy, vibrant plant. She will always remind me that sometimes we have to go into the dark to be reborn with roots deep enough to weather freeze and drought.

I sit down to meditate with rosemary. I close my eyes and imagine her blue flowers. Rosemary sounded like a strong wind blowing over a glass. Her voice was deep and rich but sailed effortlessly.

Remember.

Remember that you have all of this World and all of the other Worlds inside of you. Remember that there are lessons and stories and healing wisdoms that you already know.

Remember that there is a sweetness that opens you to these wisdoms. Remember that there is a lightness that will complement the sturdiness and reliability of these rememberings.

At that moment, the wind blew through her small strong stalks and leaves.

Rosemary embodies the spirit of remembering and teaches us to return to what we know that we may have forgotten.

LATIN:
Ruta graveolens

FAMILY:
Rutaceae

COMMON:
*Herb of Grace,
Herb of Repentance*

Rue

*There is rosemary and rue . . . Grace and
remembrance be to you.*

WILLIAM SHAKESPEARE
playwright, poet (1564–1616)

RUE IS ONE OF THE OLDEST MEDICINAL PLANTS NATIVE to the
Mediterranean. A woody evergreen perennial that survives outside
in milder winter climates, it was used in ancient times to ward off
pestilence and disease. The Romans brought ruta with them when
they invaded England and later the name was shortened to rue. The
early Roman Catholic Church sprinkled a combination of rue and
holy water as a way to cleanse sins.

Many years ago I travelled to Belize to study with Dr. Rosita
Arvigo, a world renowned ethnobotanist and herb teacher. She led
a plant walk in her garden and introduced her students to rue. I was
very attracted to the plant, and kept going over to sit near it the week
I was visiting. She explained to us that rue is used in Belize for certain
health complaints and to protect against the "evil eye" and negativity.
A sprig is often placed in a protective amulet. Dr. Arvigo lists rue in
her book, *Rainforest Remedies: One Hundred Healing Herbs of Belize.*

Rue needs to be respected, the plant contains a phytoactive chemical called psoralens. Touching the plant, especially when it is in bloom and in full sun, can cause the skin to become irritated or even blistered. I have never had any ill effects from many years of picking rue, but I know people who have. I suggest using gloves when you want to pick rue's beautiful blossoms.

Rue's yellow flowers form a cross pattern with a green dot in the center. The leaves are rounded lobes that look similar to the suit of clubs in a deck of cards. Rue adds a mysterious presence to an herbal garden.

Rue is a host plant for three varieties of Swallowtail butterflies that use this plant to lay their eggs. When they hatch the caterpillars eat many of rue's leaves. Rue doesn't seem to mind, as the leaves grow back and the plant usually survives.

Early Italian healers had rue growing by their door as a signpost that they were herbalists. To honor my Italian ancestors, I planted rue by my front door too. In 18th and 19th century Italy, a protective Italian silver charm called a cimaruta was made in the image of a sprig of rue, and sometimes hung over a baby's cradle. I like to place sprigs of rue on my altar where it adds its protective energies.

SAFETY CONSIDERATIONS: Not recommended for use during pregnancy.

MEDITATION

RUE IS MY SPECIAL PLANT ALLY and I sit on the cool ground at her feet. I smell the scent of rue rising from decaying mulch. I touch her new seedlings pushing up from the dark. I see a Swallowtail caterpillar eating her club shaped leaves and stalks. It will shroud itself in a chrysalis, attach itself to rue for protection, die into the dark. When it is reborn, its wings will carry the yellow color of rue's flowers.

I call the name of rue by chanting the "U" sound. Joseph Rael says the "U" sound is the vowel sound for carrying. Everything is vibration: music, our pulse, our name. Rue is carrying me into a deeper communion. The club-shaped leaves dance in the gentle breeze.

Rue is an ancient plant. I feel her message and she reminds me growing older is growing deeper and wiser.

I can survive the winter if the weather is not too harsh.

I pull my energy into my center for regeneration.

I pull my life force into the dark roots to be held and protected.

LATIN:
Thymus vulgaris
FAMILY:
Lamiaceae
COMMON:
Garden thyme

Thyme

I know a bank where the wild thyme blows . . .
WILLIAM SHAKESPEARE
playwright, poet (1564–1616)

NATIVE TO THE MEDITARRANEAN REGION AND CULTIVATED worldwide, thyme has about 400 species. It is a culinary herb that blends well with rosemary, oregano and marjoram. Its leaves are evergreen and it is a perennial plant that likes well-drained soil.

In the middle of winter the evergreen thyme leaves can be found in my garden. If you have sinus congestion, heat some water in a pot and infuse fresh or dried thyme leaves. Cover your head with a towel and breath in the steam from the leaves. Thyme tea helps to relieve coughs, sore throats and phlegm. It has antiviral and antibacterial properties.

Although thyme has delicate, tiny flowers and leaves, do not be fooled by its appearance. It has strong antiseptic qualities. The antimicrobial effects of the essential oil has been used in aromatherapy diffusers to help clear germs. Thymol, one of the chemical components of thyme, is being used in many cleaning products.

In Shakespeare's play, *A Midsummer Night's Dream*, Titania, the Queen of the fairies sleeps on a bank of wild thyme. Carrying a sprig of thyme is said to help you gain a glimpse into the land of the fairies. Try putting a sprig in your pocket as you walk in the woods.

SAFETY CONSIDERATIONS: Avoid applying thyme essential oil on the skin during pregnancy. Safe to use as a culinary herb during pregnancy.

MEDITATION

AS I SAT WITH THYME, I heard the whisper of a grandmother.

Grandchild, you know how I love you?

I will love and protect you through time.

When you need me,

Call on me.

You will find me in the garden's nooks and crannies.

The love that I have for you is forever.

You may tell your children and they may tell their children's children.

Other Meditation Practices

lants assist humanity not only with physical, emotional, and mental well-being, but also with spiritual well-being. Like bees drawn to the nectar of the flower, we too are sometimes drawn to a certain plant because we feel a resonance with its vibration and it carries a healing attribute we need.

LIGHT BODY

THE ENERGY BODY OR LIGHT BODY HAS BEEN referenced across many cultures throughout history. It is a term that is used to define the energy body that is a template for the physical, emotional, mental, and spiritual bodies. Plants, animals, and humans all have light bodies.

Our light bodies extend far beyond our physical bodies and hold the blueprint for our multidimensional self. This part of our being can travel beyond time and space. We often access our light body while dreaming.

We carry our light body as an energetic form. Sometimes the light body is described as the imprint of the Soul. Anyone who has taken or created a flower essence understands how flowers carry the energetic form of the plant as we carry the energetic form of our souls.

When two living beings come together, their light bodies interact. Potentially their light bodies may resonate with one another in a harmonious way. When two waves of light resonate harmoniously, the energy expands and becomes stronger. If the light waves are not in harmony with each other, they can essentially mute each other.

A loving connection between you and a plant can begin through the subtle frequency of the light body once you bring awareness to it. Plants have a special connection to light with their ability to make their own food from the energy of the sun.

To enter into a light body meditation with a plant partner takes patience and practice. We suggest you meditate for at least twenty to thirty minutes.

Visualize spiraling into the dark earth around the plant's roots and then imagine yourself merging with the plant's roots. Feel yourself being drawn up from the roots through the branches and stems into the plant's bright green leaves. Feel yourself drinking light with the leaves from the life-giving energy of the sun. Feel the healing light flowing through you to all the cells of your body.

You may want to journal your impressions afterwards.

SITTING ON THE EARTH MEDITATION
~ Paulette ~

ONE OF THE EARLY PLANTS I CONNECTED TO IN THE GARDEN is a plant called rue. Rue is a mysterious plant and has been used for protection and magic for centuries.

I touched the leaves, and the scent of rue released, pungent but still pleasant. I tasted a tiny bit of rue's bitter leaves. Rue's small, yellow flowers attract bees, and I watched them swarm around the leaves and stems. I sat beside rue, listening to her vibration.

I sat with my sacrum directly touching the earth, and felt energy move through me. I felt roots growing from my sacrum reaching deep into the soil. At this moment I felt as if I were breathing with the earth. It was a shock to feel this power as I inhaled and exhaled.

I remembered a yoga meditation I learned once for running energy from the root chakra up through the solar plexus; then to the heart, throat, and crown chakras; and then sending the energy through the pineal gland in the brain and down the spine to the sacrum and into the earth. I thought this practice might be a good way to prepare to meditate with my plant ally, rue.

A caterpillar was feeding on the leaves of rue. Its yellow stripes matched the color of rue's yellow flowers so well, I needed to look carefully to see it. The caterpillar would feed until it wove itself a shroud where its own body would be food for its transforming self. Could our own human lives be the food for our own transformation?

This caterpillar would become a swallowtail butterfly that would carry the yellow and green colors of rue into the form of a delicate and beautiful butterfly. The butterfly would dance flower to flower, carrying pollen and fertility around this garden and to the next.

As I inhaled, I felt my light body connect to rue and received a message from the plant. Rue said, I am medicine and each individual is medicine to each other, and we must take care to use our medicine wisely.

HEART CHAKRA MEDITATION
~ Judith ~

CHAKRAS ARE SUBTLE CENTERS IN OUR BODIES THAT HELP with balancing our energies and emotions. Unconditional love, compassion for yourself as well as others, and feelings of joy are attributes of the heart chakra. The color associated with the heart chakra is the soothing color of green found in nature.

To begin this meditation, you may want to place your hand over your heart and connect to your own heart center. Ask to be released of any self-imposed limiting beliefs or fears. Imagine yourself surrounded with love and compassion.

Then ask permission from the plant to connect with it. Once you feel a connection to yourself and the plant, send your grounding cord deeply into the core of the earth.

From your heart chakra in the center of your chest, send a beam of green light to the plant. Look at the flowers, leaves and stems;

visualize the roots in the earth. Feel the green light from your heart chakra connecting with the plant's green energy. Bring your awareness to the whole plant.

Begin to chant the name of the plant and chant for as long as you wish. You can also sit in silence with the plant.

When you feel complete, gently disconnect the beam of green light and thank the plant. Take several breaths and return to the present moment. Journal any images or messages you receive.

Asarum arifolium, HEARTLEAF GINGER

DREAMING
~ Judith ~

AS WE EXPAND OUR RELATIONSHIP WITH THE GARDEN and plants, there is a greater potential to start dreaming about nature. Helping the mind and body to relax and enter a deeper state of sleep is important to dreaming. I like to place a flower or sprig of a favorite plant near my bed and breathe in the aromatic scent of the herb as I go to sleep. Mugwort, *Artemisia vulgaris* is a plant known to enhance dreaming. A sachet of dried mugwort can be placed near one's pillow. Sometimes a drop or two of an essential oil like lavender, rose, chamomile, or vetiver on the pillowcase can help with relaxation. You can also diffuse the oils in an aromatherapy diffuser.

I keep a dream journal by my bed and upon awakening, I write the dream in my journal. Dreams can be elusive, and a few key words or phrases can help you remember your dream. After recalling a dream, use your intuition to interpret the dream; sometimes the dream's message will slowly reveal itself. Sharing the dream with a friend can be helpful.

I recently dreamt about the earth. In the dream I was in a dark cave that had an opening in the ceiling where I could see the night sky and a few stars. It reminded me of the sacred caves I used to visit in New Mexico. I heard a woman's voice say in Spanish, "La madre tierra canta." Translated it means, "The mother earth sings." I heard a deep humming sound that resonated inside the peaceful cave, which sounded like "mmmm" and had a healing quality to it. The sound was like the collective buzzing of bees in the garden. I woke up still feeling the soothing hum in my body. Whether it be crickets, bees, or a breeze rustling the leaves, the earth is singing her song.

AFTER READING ABOUT THE VARIOUS PRACTICES, you may be wondering how to get started. You don't have to have a garden; you can start with going for a walk and sitting with a plant you find.

You may find this plant in a meadow, forest or in your yard. If you are new to being with plants use a plant field guide or go on a walk with an herbalist who can help you learn to identify plants. Plantain, dandelion, chickweed and other plants that are sometimes called 'weeds' often grow right in your lawn. If you live in a city, find a botanical garden where you can connect with a plant.

Disconnect from electronic devices so you are not interrupted. Plan on thirty minutes to get comfortable and meditate. Feel the earth under your feet as deep roots grounding and connecting you with the earth's energy. Be as present as you can be in the moment with no judgement towards yourself. Be with the plant and see what is revealed to you.

Everyone's journey with plants is personal and individual. Connecting with plants is like having a conversation. Some conversations are joyful, some humorous and others deep and profound. The way you enter this conversation can take many forms. For some it will be through chanting, or for others, meditating. For some it might be playing a drum or singing bowl, painting, drawing, or journaling.

Flower Essences

~ Judith ~

lower essences are made with flowers picked with gratitude, spring water and sunlight. An energetic imprint of the flower's healing properties is made by infusing the flowers into the water. From this water, gentle remedies are made that work throughout the energetic field of the body, especially with our thoughts, feelings and emotions.

Dr. Edward Bach (1886–1936) was an English physician and a pioneer of flower essence therapy. Through his research he found that flower essences could help heal emotional imbalances and he developed thirty-eight vibrational remedies that correspond to specific emotional states. His remedies and research are still being used today.

To make your own personal essence, start with a plant that you know well, that you feel a connection with and that you know is a safe plant. The first essence I made many years ago was with a wild white rose that grew by my house. I took the rose essence over several weeks and felt its nurturing vibration balancing my emotions.

In preparation for making any flower essence, begin by observing the plant's physical characteristics; its color, patterns, the shape of its flower and leaves. Carefully observing the plant's habitats will tell you a lot about its qualities. Does the plant like sun, shade, or a mixture of both? Does it like to grow by water, or does it like well-drained soil? When you make a new friend, you get to know their characteristics: who they are--their likes and dislikes. It is the same when getting to know your plants.

Speak out loud to the plant about your intentions to make an essence and ask permission. Sometimes we have sensed from the plants that it wasn't the right day to harvest the flowers. Allow your intuition to guide you in this process.

When we look at a plant we are often drawn to the color and beauty of its flowers. Herbalists from many traditions feel flowers are communicating their healing properties with their shape, design pattern, and colors. This has been referred to as the Doctrine of Signatures.

MAKING A FLOWER ESSENCE

WHAT YOU WILL NEED:

- a clear glass bowl or a crystal bowl
- clean scissors or tweezers
- spring water
- brandy
- wooden spoon or chopsticks
- funnel

Use a clear glass bowl without words, as the words can imprint on the water.

It is optimal to make your flower essences on a sunny day. You will want to pick the flowers in the early morning, when the flowers are open and may have morning dew on them. It is optimal if there is dew on the flowers, though in some climates and seasons there will be no dew. Some flower essences are made at night with the light of the full moon.

A BORAGE FLOWER ESSENCE

STEPS TO MAKING A FLOWER ESSENCE

🌿 Fill the bowl with water, six to twelve ounces is fine. The amount of water you use depends on how much essence you want to make, and how many flowers you have. If you have only a few flowers, consider using a smaller bowl and less water.

As Masura Emoto says, "We must pay respect to water, and feel love and gratitude. Then, water changes, you change, and I change. Because you and I are water" (145).

🌿 Ground and center yourself, and speak your gratitudes to the plant. Carefully cut the flower blossoms close to the base of the flower with your scissors or tweezers.

🌿 Place the flowers facing up into the bowl of water about one layer deep so that the flowers are floating on the surface of the water. If you only have a few flowers the essence can still be made.

🌿 You can pray or state your intentions for the flower essence to reach its highest healing potential in this time and space.

A ROSEMARY FLOWER ESSENCE

🌿 Set the bowl filled with flowers in the garden near the plant. It is best if the essence is not shaded while the sun moves across the sky; should the weather become cloudy the essence can still be made with the available light.

🌿 The water is receiving an energetic imprint from the flower blossoms.

Let the flowers infuse in the bowl of water for around three to four hours. Let your intuition guide you as to when the essence is complete.

🌿 When the essence is complete, carefully remove the flowers using a clean wooden spoon, chopsticks or a leaf. Do not use your hands, as you may contaminate the essence. Return any plant material to the earth with gratitude.

🌿 Whatever amount of essence you have, use an equal amount of brandy to preserve it. For example, to six ounces of the flower essence you will add six ounces of brandy (organic if available). This is a 50:50 mother essence dilution.

🍃 Using a funnel, pour this into a sterilized glass bottle. I prefer amber glass bottles, as they help protect the essence from UV light.

🍃 Label the mother essence bottle with the name, date and location of where the essence was made. You can also add the words, love or gratitude to the label. Over many years of research, Masura Emoto found that water responds best to the words, "love and gratitude."

🍃 Store your mother essence in a dark cabinet, it will be preserved for many years.

MAKING A STOCK ESSENCE

MAKE A STOCK ESSENCE BY ADDING 10 drops from the mother essence to a two ounce or 60 milliliters mL. bottle. To preserve the stock essence again add a 50:50 dilution of spring water with brandy and gently tap the bottom of the bottle to mix. Label this clearly as a stock essence with name and date.

If you are taking a flower essence remedy, take two to three drops of the flower essence directly from a stock bottle. Gently tap the bottom of the stock bottle to energize the essence before taking it.

Flower essence practitioners may futher dilute the flower essence or they might combine several flower essences to create a dosage bottle for their client.

MAKING A DOSAGE BOTTLE

TO MAKE A DOSAGE BOTTLE FROM YOUR STOCK ESSENCE, use a clean one ounce or 30 milliliters ml bottle. Add four drops from the stock bottle to your clean bottle. Fill the bottle (3/4) full of spring water and top off the rest with brandy to preserve the essence. Gently tap the bottom of the bottle to energize the essence.

If you are sensitive to alcohol consider using apple cider vinegar or vegetable glycerin to preserve your essence.

SUGGESTIONS FOR TAKING A FLOWER ESSENCE: place three drops under the tongue, three times a day for up to several weeks. You can also add three drops to a glass of water. Gently stir the water and sip.

Flower essences can also be added to a bath. Water conducts electromagnetic energy. While sitting in a bath, the patterns of energy that are held in the body may be benefited by the vibration of the flower essence. Add three drops to your bath water.

There are many wonderful flower essence companies. They usually have detailed information on the energetic properties of each essence they carry. Essences are made in different regions of the world and carry the vibration of the place they are made. See resources for more information on flower essence companies.

Flower essences make a unique contribution to the emotional and spiritual health of people and some essences are made specifically for animals such as dogs and cats.

There are flower essence practitioners that can help you with choosing the right essence for your particular life situation.

Plants are the essence of angels in physical form.

DR. ROSITA ARVIGO
master herbalist (1941–)

FLOWER BATHING

~ Judith ~

OVER SEVERAL YEARS I TRAVELLED TO BELIZE TO STUDY with Dr. Rosita Arvigo, who is a napropathic physician, author and master herbalist. Dr. Arvigo teaches the principles of bathing using plants, prayers, water and incense during the course of a five day retreat. This spiritual practice can help release anxiety, stress and worry and cleanses one's energy body. Bathing rituals are done in many cultures worldwide and I refer you to her wonderful book called *Spiritual Bathing*.

From my experience, bathing with your favorite plants is a way to nurture yourself and uplift your mood. Pick the flowers and leaves you want to use with permission from the plant. I speak out loud to the plants as I connect with them stating my gratitude and appreciation for them.

There are many plants to choose from such as calendula, lavender, rose, peony, dandelion, violet, marigold, mint, thyme, oregano, marjoram, holy basil and culinary basil, sage and plantain leaves to name a few. Use your intuition to guide you to the plants you need in your bath. Avoid plants that may have been sprayed with chemicals. If you are not sure of the identity or safety of a flower or plant, please do some research or don't use it. Going on a plant walk with a local herbalist is one way to learn about plant safety.

Create a bathing ritual for yourself. You may want to light a candle, burn incense, and play some soothing music. You can use the flower water in your shower, bath or outside if you have a space. After a flower bath you may feel a sense of renewal and peace. I suggest taking the plant material outside if possible and giving it back to the earth in gratitude. If you wish to learn more about this healing practice, consider taking a class with the Abdominal Therapy Collective. See resources.

Herbal Basics and Recipes

~ *Judith* ~

here are many books and on-line classes on how to make herbal medicine. Some are listed in our resources section. We share some basic herbal terms and a few favorite recipes from the plants in this book.

Herbal teas are another way to connect with the healing energies of the plants. If you are going to make a tea with fresh herbs that you have picked; remember to ask permission first. You can also use dried herbs. While you are sipping your herbal tea take the time to notice the tea's flavors. Does the tea taste bitter, sweet, sour or pungent? Do you feel calm and relaxed or more energized after drinking the tea? Pay attention to any sensations you are feeling in your body. Close your eyes and relax in meditation.

If you are gathering herbs to make tea, please remember a few principles of harvesting plants. Never take all of the leaves from one plant. Harvest leaves from several plants and leave enough leaves so the plant can grow back. Also leave some flowers for the pollinators, the bees, insects and hummingbirds. If you are out in the wild collecting plants, and there are only a few plants available, consider not picking from the area. Let the plants continue to grow undisturbed. Be considerate and respectful of the plants.

- fresh or dried herbs, barks, or roots (see below for specific steps for each recipe)
- a teapot or non-aluminum cooking pot, or a canning jar
- muslin, cheesecloth, or strainer
- spring water or well water
- alcohol (vodka, brandy, or rum)
- vegetable glycerin
- drying screen or (optional) dehydrator

HERBAL TEAS

HERBAL TEAS CONTAIN VITAMINS AND MINERALS and are nourishing to the body. Easy to prepare, they can be made with fresh or dried plants.

HOW TO MAKE A TEA INFUSION

Fresh herbs already contain water, so double the amount of fresh plant material in an infusion so that your infusion is not diluted. We use a canning jar to make an infusion, as the glass is not prone to crack from the heat. A teapot or non-aluminum cooking pot also works well.

- Steep 1-2 teaspoons (1 teaspoon equals 5.00 milliliters mL) of dried leaves or flowers to one cup of boiling water.
- Steep 2-4 teaspoons of fresh herbs to one cup of boiling water.
- Once the water has boiled, let it sit for a moment, as boiling hot water will dissipate the volatile oils of the fresh plants. Pour the hot water over the herbs.
- Cover with a lid and let steep for 10-20 minutes. If you want to make a stronger infusion, let the herbs sit overnight in the jar or tea pot.

🌿 Strain the herbs through muslin, cheesecloth, or strainer and refrigerate. The infusion will keep for up to two to three days.

HOW TO MAKE AN HERBAL DECOCTION

TO MAKE A DECOCTION, USE FRESH OR DRIED HERBS, ROOTS, or barks. Simmer the plant material in water. The simmering process extracts more of the healing constituents than an infusion does.

🌿 Place 1 ounce of dried or 2 ounces of fresh herbs in 32 ounces of cold water, or 30 grams of dried herbs to one liter of cold water.

🌿 Simmer in a cooking pot for twenty minutes to one hour until the liquid is reduced by one third to one half in volume.

🌿 Strain the herbs through muslin, cheesecloth or strainer. Refrigerate.

The herbal liquid can be kept in a refrigerator for two to three days.

DRYING HERBS

IT IS LOVELY TO MAKE TEAS FROM THE PLANTS YOU GROW in your garden or garden pots. It is best to pick the leaves on a sunny day when the plant is completely dry. Pick the freshest leaves of the plant not using any leaves that have turned brown. Generally you harvest herbs before the flowers open. Drying culinary and medicinal herbs is a way to enjoy herbs, especially in the winter time when fresh herbs may be hard to find. Once you get a drying system in place it is a fun project to do in the summer.

There are several methods you can use to dry herbs. One is to create a drying screen. To make a drying screen, stretch either nylon screening or muslin cloth over a wooden frame. You can then set several screens on a drying rack or create a more permanent drying cupboard to set the screens in. Set the screens in a well ventilated room or with a fan on to promote air circulation. Drying herbs out of the direct sunlight is important, as the light can degrade the medicinal properties of the herbs.

You can also invest in a dehydrator. Many dehydrators have a setting for herbs which is 105° F or 41°C.

Climate makes a difference in drying herbs. North Carolina has a very humid climate and leaves and flowers will take longer to dry. Drying herbs in an arid climate like New Mexico is a different experience as the herbs can dry quickly.

Different plants have different drying times based on the thickness of the leaves and the amount of water and essential oils found in the leaves. Good ventilation is important. For example, holy basil leaves take less time to dry than calendula flowers. Holy basil leaves will feel crisp when they are completely dry.

Calendula flowers have a sticky resinous green base called a calyx, which is part of calendula's medicine. It can take ten or more hours to dry calendula in a dehydrator. I check on the herbs several times during the drying process.

You want the herbs to be completely dry before storing them. I have had herbs mold in a jar because they were not fully dry. I place the herbs in a brown paper bag for a week or so before transferring them to a clean glass jar. Store the jars in a cabinet or pantry out of the sunlight.

You can also tie small bundles of plants and hang them with the leaves pointing down, in a well ventilated area. A rubber band can be used to tie the herbs up in bundles. As the stems of the plants dry, the rubber band keeps the herbs together. When the plants are dry, take the leaves off the stems and branches, crush the herbs, (it creates more space in the bag). Place them in a brown paper bag for a while, before transferring to a clean glass jar. Enjoy the harvest!

TINCTURE

A TINCTURE IS AN EXTRACT OF MEDICINAL PLANTS, ROOTS, or barks made with a menstruum, which is the liquid solvent used to extract the herbs. Examples of a menstruum are alcohol, apple cider vinegar and vegetable glycerin. Alcohol is often used because more of the plant's healing properties are extracted with alcohol than water. If possible use organic alcohol or organic apple cider vinegar.

An alcohol tincture can be made with vodka because it doesn't change the flavor of the herbs. Brandy or rum can also be used, because of the flavor it conveys to the tincture. The process of extracting herbs with a solvent such as alcohol is called a maceration extract. If organic alcohol is available and affordable consider using it instead.

HOW TO MAKE A SIMPLE TINCTURE

BELOW IS A SIMPLE METHOD FOR TINCTURING HERBS from your garden. There are more complex methods that involve further study.

- To begin you may want to ground and center yourself, and speak your intentions and gratitudes to the plants.

- If you are gathering fresh leaves, pick them on a sunny day in the afternoon, when there is no moisture on the plants.

- If you are gathering roots, wash the dirt off with plain water (no soap).

- Chop and dry the roots in a dehydrator before tincturing them, as the tincture will contain less water when the roots are dry. You can also dry the roots on a screen with good air circulation.

- Chop the plant material up in small pieces that will fit in a jar. One of the best jars to use is a wide-mouthed glass canning jar with a tight screw-down lid, one that won't corrode from being in contact with the alcohol.

- Cover the plant material with the alcohol or vegetable glycerin, tamp the herbs down with a chopstick releasing any air bubbles. Leave a headspace of two to three inches at the top of the jar.

- Close the jar tightly. Store in a dark pantry for four weeks, shaking the jar every day. Check on the tincture after shaking the jar making sure the plant material is submerged in the alcohol.

- Strain and press the plant material through several layers of cheesecloth or a clean cloth like muslin. The plant material that remains after the extraction is called the marc, which can be composted. Pour the tincture into a clean sterile jar.

- Label your jar with the name, date, and menstruum used.

- Store your tinctures away from sunlight in a cabinet. The tinctures can be kept for several years if they are correctly stored.

ELDERBERRY SYRUP RECIPE

THIS DELICIOUS SYRUP CAN BE ENJOYED YEAR ROUND. You can add a few spoonfuls of syrup to hot water to make tea. Remember that raw elderberries and green stems can cause gastric distress, so don't eat raw berries.

What you will need:

- Fresh or dried elderberries organic if possible.
- Local honey
- Optional cinnamon stick
- Cooking pot
- Clean sterile jar and lid
- Label

- Place one cup or 100 grams of dried or fresh berries in a non-aluminum cooking pot. Cover with two cups of water. Add an optional cinnamon stick. Some people prefer just the flavor of elderberry.
- Cover and allow to simmer on low heat until the liquid mixture reduces by half. Stir frequently.
- Let the mixture cool so it is easier to handle.
- Strain it through a fine sieve strainer or layers of cheesecloth and press the liquid out of the berries into a clean jar.
- Compost the remaining elderberries and seeds.
- Measure the amount of concentrated elderberry liquid, which will be approximately one cup of liquid. Pour the elderberry liquid back into the cooking pot and reheat till it's warm.
- To the one cup of the warm elderberry concentrate, add one cup of honey. Stir until the honey dissolves.
- Pour into a clean sterilized glass jar. Create a label with a date your syrup was made.
- Store your syrup in the refrigerator. It will keep for several months. Shake well before using.

INFUSED OILS

HERBS CAN BE INFUSED INTO ORGANIC OILS SUCH AS OLIVE oil, sweet almond, avocado, or sunflower oil and used externally on the skin. The oils can be used for massage, skin care or made into a salve. We suggest using organic oils, as the body will absorb any chemicals or pesticides that are in the oils. Infused herbal oils are not the same as essential oils which are made with steam distillation.

Herbal oils can be made from fresh or dried plants. There is a risk to using fresh plant material as the oil can mold because of the water content in the plant. Partially drying the plants or wilting the leaves overnight reduces the water content and there is a less chance of the oil molding.

Some plants like calendula are always used dried in an infused oil. Plantain is wilted to let some of the water in the plant evaporate.

There are some exceptions, such as using only fresh mullein flowers to make an infused mullein oil. Check with a plant medicine making book for more information.

What you will need to make an infused oil:

- various plant material
- a carrier oil (organic olive, sunflower or avocado oil)
- a clean cloth
- a clean sterilized jar
- clean chopstick or spoon
- cheesecloth

PLANTAIN OIL RECIPE

PLANTAIN OIL HAS ANTI-INFLAMMATORY AND anti-bacterial properties. It can be used for bruises, skin irritations, abrasions, insect bites, and eczema. I like to make this oil in the springtime when the leaves are vibrant and before the plant has gone to seed.

- Ground and ask permission from the plantain plants and offer your thanks. Pick the plantain leaves on a dry sunny afternoon when the plants are completely dry. It is best to have no dew on the plants as you don't want to add any extra moisture. Extra moisture will spoil the infused oil.

- Plantain is best gathered in a clean location. Don't gather plantain or any other herbs near the edge of the road where there may be pollution or chemical contaminants.

- Bring the harvested leaves inside and place them on a clean cloth. Let the leaves wilt overnight. The wilting process allows the moisture to leave the plant, the less moisture, the better chance the oil won't mold.

- Cut the leaves into one to two-inch pieces on a clean cutting board and place in a clean dry jar. Pack the jar 2/3 full with the plantain leaves. Completely cover the plantain with a carrier oil like olive oil, avocado oil or sunflower oil. Use organic oils when possible.

- Take a clean chopstick or spoon and gently tamp the leaves down, releasing any air bubbles out of the oil. Add more oil so there is at least one inch of oil covering all of the plant material.

- Tightly cap the jar and set it on a windowsill where it will absorb the healing light from the sun and the moon for around four weeks. This solar method works best when using dry herbs. With partially dry herbs there is a risk mold will grow.

- Check on the oil infusion frequently.

- The oil is a vibrant green color when it is complete.

- Strain the oil through several layers of cheesecloth and place the oil in a clean jar. Cover the jar with a lid and let it sit overnight. There will be plant material that will settle to the bottom of the jar, so strain it again through several layers of cheesecloth into another clean jar.

- Compost the sludgy plant material on the bottom of the jar.

- Label and date the jar, and store in the refrigerator for up to one year.

DOUBLE BOILER METHOD FOR MAKING INFUSED OIL

What you will need:

- Double boiler

- Candy Thermometer

- Premade mixture of plant material and oil

I use the stovetop method for making calendula oil as I find the heat helps to extract the medicinal oil from the dried calendula flowers. I have also used this method to make plantain oil. When you need your infused oil and can't wait four weeks, we suggest the stove top—double boiler method. Start with heating water in the bottom pan of a double boiler until it is simmering. Then pour your plant mixture and oil into the top of the double boiler pan. Keep the watering simmering in the bottom pan and check on the water levels often. Use your thermometer to check the temperature of the oil keeping it around 110 degrees. Infuse your oil for about six hours. When complete, strain the oil through several layers of cheesecloth. Label and date your jar. Store in the refrigerator for one year.

Teachings from our Elders

Over the years we have been blessed with many teachings from our elders and friends. To honor those teachings we have added a few of their stories and notes taken from our journals.

JOURNEY TO MOUNTAIN GARDENS
~ *Paulette* ~

IT IS JUNE OF 2019 AND JUDITH AND I ARE TRAVELING to the mountains for a weeklong writing retreat and also to take a class with Joe Hollis at Mountain Gardens near Burnsville, North Carolina. Joe has been on the land for about forty years, teaching many students how to identify, cultivate, harvest and prepare medicinal herbs. His four-acre plant nursery and garden has over 500 species of Chinese herbs and native plants and trees.

Mountain Gardens is near one of the highest mountain ranges on the eastern seaboard of North America. During the last ice age, many species didn't survive the glaciers sweeping down from the north, but this part of the Black Mountain range was protected, and many species survived. He compares the climate in a part of Asia with the climate in Western North Carolina. Many Chinese herbs do well here.

Joe's gardens are on a steep piece of mountain land bordering the Pisgah National Forest. He and his apprentices have terraced the garden over many, many years. It is starting to rain, but we are ready with our boots and raincoats for the plant walk. It has been raining most of the week and the paths and plant beds are soggy with mud.

Joe, like me, is in his seventies but is very nimble. I watch him leap from a terraced bed to a creek bank. As he moves among the plants, he becomes more animated. It's as if each plant were reaching out to him saying, "Pick me."

He begins by pointing out wild perennial vegetables that come up every year. He grows air potato vines in tubes because their roots are fragile and hard to pull out of the ground. Many people see this vine as a weed. I taste the root; it is delicate and mild. Rudolph Steiner listed this "weed" as an important food plant.

Joe shows us other perennial edibles. Violets are high in Vitamin C. The immature flowers of milkweed taste like broccoli. He has us try the tender tips of the cleaver plant, and creasy greens that are in the mustard family.

He is growing sochan, which is a native plant the Cherokee used as an important spring edible. Sochan is a yellow-petaled flower with a green center that is related to coneflowers. Judith has sochan growing in her garden, a plant she got from Joe more than 10 years ago. I didn't know that you could cook the tender spring sochan leaves and that they are chock-full of folic acid and minerals.

We learn that Joe has been invited to speak at a conference in Switzerland on perennial vegetables and foraging wild plants. Europe is becoming drier because of climate change and the conference focused on the importance of perennial vegetables and wild foods as a food source.

The rain is coming down heavier now and the slippery path is getting too treacherous for me. I decide to leave the group and go back to his library, a rustic building filled with shelves of botanical volumes. In an adjacent room, is the apothecary, where brown bottles of tinctures and dried herbs line the walls.

I find an album of pictures of the early days of Mountain Garden. Within the album is a yellowed piece of paper with typing from an old manual typewriter.

The unknown author speaks of how we all need gardens. How we need them not for beauty alone but also to get closer to who we are. To this purpose, gardens are wild and diverse things, not something tidy or controlled. In gardens we can be natural, ourselves, taking our place to sit and study, work and play, and to listen to the messages of plants.

I was inspired by the depth of knowledge Joe Hollis possesses. He has an encyclopedic store of information as well as a lifetime of careful observation and experience. Mountain Gardens is extraordinary, and I will never forget my visit there.

THE BEE CALLER
~ *Francis Rico* ~

I LIVE WITH ARTIST DODI O'NEILL AND AT THE CENTER of our garden in California is a small natural stone altar. Every year a bountiful spray of holy basil plants make their home with lush, green growth in its nooks and crannies.

As altars always seem to do, this one has grown over time to include everything from crystals and special rocks brought home from travels, to a little cast bell from the Sacred Valley in Peru.

Along with a sense of natural sacredness that exists at the heart of the garden my partner, Dodi, and I share a love for the eternal paradise that gardens innately are. We both have special feelings of affection for certain plants. It's something that every gardener knows: plants also grow in our hearts.

To see the care and attention that Dodi brings to the needs of each plant in our garden is touching. We have as many wildflowers and plants for hummingbirds and bees as we have vegetables and herbs. Many of what others call "weeds" are welcomed and cared for. She calls them "volunteers."

One of Dodi's ways of getting to know a plant is to get up very close and personal with a sketchpad. Her sketches note every intimate detail of a plant's structure and personality. One day I noticed that she seemed particularly pleased with her sketch of holy basil, and it just seemed normal when I saw her turn the sketch around to show the plant her work, as if to say, "See how beautiful you are?"

I have my ways of appreciating beauty in the garden, starting with a morning ceremony to greet each new day. I go to the altar and ring the little bell. The sweet fragrant smell of holy basil is intense as bees swarm in surrounding me and the plants.

Plants must love ceremonies too, because every morning the holy basil seemed to respond with a more vibrant glow and with a more intensely aromatic scent of fresh sweetness. It delighted me to think of myself as a bee caller--calling all bees in to celebrate the morning!

I happened to mention bee calling to my friend Paulette. She had just learned that plants respond to the vibration of bees' wings by increasing their sweet nectar scent, thereby calling in the bees.

Entering into the sacred at the heart of our garden, I slipped into the conversation that holy basil was already having with the bees. The tiny bell was welcomed by the plants just as if it were the beating of bee wings, and the plants in turn called in the bees with their nectar and pollen.

By becoming part of nature's conversation, I joined with the intrinsic magic of the natural world. I better understood the relationship Dodi shares with each plant she gets to know as she paints its portrait.

I could still call myself a bee caller, but I know better. It is the holy basil and the bees that are calling me to the beauty at the heart of the garden!

OUR ANCESTORS AS HERBALISTS
~ Judith ~

Without our ancestors, we would not be here in our physical form. I am grateful for what I learned from my parents and grandmothers about gardening as a child. They enjoyed growing herbs and vegetables and would make me a cup of herbal tea when I was sick. Think about your own family? Did you have a grandparent or elder who knew how to prepare herbs for a cough or cold?

The use of herbal medicine is common to all people and cultures on the earth. Knowledge of plant medicine was passed down as an oral tradition through generations of families. Many European and Indigenous healers were women who prepared herbal medicine for the sick in their family or village. They were the wise women, who knew the herbs to help with labor and birth. They used their knowledge to help heal.

As Europeans immigrated and settled throughout the continents, they brought plants and their herbal knowledge with them. American Indians had an extensive knowledge of the plants, roots and barks of North America. They shared their knowledge with the Europeans. Sadly, these settlers also carried deadly diseases such as smallpox, that decimated the native populations of North and South America and Africa. Millions of indigenous people around the world suffered and died from diseases which they had no immunity to.

Slave ships from West Africa brought seeds and plants with them as part of the slave trade. African slaves also shared their knowledge of plants and through oral traditions as they were cruelly denied the right to learn to read or write. African traditional medicine, which includes herbalism and spiritualism, have all contributed to our contemporary knowledge of herbalism ("Slave Medicine").

A cultural overview of herbalism spans every continent and nation. A few herbal traditions are listed here. Ayurvedic medicine has its roots in India. Curanderos and Maya traditional healers come from the Yucatec region of Mexico. The Unani system of medicine has its roots in Islam. Chinese medicine comes from China and other parts of Asia. These traditions contribute to our planetary knowledge of herbal medicine.

PLANTS AS ELDERS
~ Judith ~

Plants have been on the planet for almost 500 million years. In terms of evolution, they are our elders. Sometimes when you meet a plant for the first time you may feel drawn to the smell of its flowers or the color of its blossoms or shape of its leaves. A suggestion is to start with one plant, sit beside it, and get to know it. You may feel a sense of openness and joy when you are around a plant ally.

If the plant is edible, consider tasting it. The taste of the plant can often be felt in different systems of the body. You may feel it in your heart or chest, digestive system, or you may feel clearer mentally. Organoleptic study involves using the senses, especially tasting and smelling an herb, to understand its medicinal uses. You may be drawn to the taste of the plant and intuitively know this plant would be helpful for you to drink as a tea.

A special time to connect with a plant is at sunrise. Plants can sense when sunrise is coming and some species like sunflowers gradually turn their leaves towards the sun. Plants start the process of photosynthesis at dawn. I often enjoy sunrise while sitting in the garden, watching as the sunlight touches the plants' leaves.

Connect with the plants during the cycles of the moon, especially the full moon. Sitting in your garden under the light of the full moon is a special, magical time to be with the plants.

Having a plant ally is similar to having a spirit guide; both are there to support you in your healing journey. Spirit guides come from the spirit realms and sometimes they can be healthy ancestors who are wanting to assist us. One can have a variety of plant allies during your lifetime. Some plants show up during a time of a life transition, when extra support is needed.

Plants follow a cyclical path of nature: of birth, life, death, and regeneration. We too are a part of this life cycle. We can enter this conversation with nature and realize the miracle of this connection.

TEACHINGS ON THE DRUM
~ *Zoe Allison-Rockingbear* ~

WILL ROCKINGBEAR (1935–2013) WAS A RESPECTED Cherokee elder and teacher who lived in the mountains of North Carolina. We asked his wife and companion to share a teaching on the drum.

I look forward to looking in your eyes and celebrating with you this ancient ceremony of working with the drum and calling in your own helpers, guides, protectors, and ancestors. Our ancestors have been enjoying this part of the creation of personal medicine since the beginning of sound. Our spiritual ceremonies have always led to ways to contact Creator directly and get the attention of the spirits we work with. I hope that you will consider working with the teachings around the drum to create a container for the great Central Drum.

The different beats of the drum with your songs will always serve you well. The connections you have with the Great Mystery starts with the blending of your voice and the drum. The heartbeat of Mother Earth responds easily as you learn to recognize your part in this active healing of ourselves and Mother Earth.

THE NEW WORLD
~ *Joseph Rael* ~

WE ARE ENTERING A NEW RELATIONSHIP WITH ALL BEINGS
and it is called the Fifth world, which is Pah-nu in the Tiwa language.

As you come to this New World
I ask you to come with respect.
I mean respect for all things,
respecting the divine presence of
the Tree of Life, for this is our
family tree, our world tree, of all
the families of all the eternities.

JOSEPH RAEL
BEAUTIFUL PAINTED ARROW
BEING AND VIBRATION: ENTERING THE NEW WORLD
(1935–)

Conclusion

This beautiful blue planet is our only home.

DALAI LAMA
(1935–)

~ *Paulette* ~

In the years since Judith and I planted our first garden, the garden has taught me many things. I learned to pay attention and listen. I learned that plants communicate in their own language, and I learned a little of that language. I learned to place my hands in the earth and not be afraid of what I might find there. I learned to ask the plant before I pick its flower or stem and to leave a gift in exchange for what I take.

I am an elder, a mother, and grandmother, and this land is part of my heritage. This place is where my mother grew food for our family, planted flowers, and created beauty with a garden. I understand this desire for beauty and connection with the natural world, and have come to believe we are co-creators with nature and the land.

I want to see all our grandchildren and great-grandchildren grow up in a world where there is clean water, where the air is fresh, and where we walk on the earth with respect and appreciation.

I have learned about the unexpected journeys that come with friendship. I am grateful to my friend Judith for bringing her knowledge and passion on this journey of creating this book.

Over time our garden has come to recognize our footsteps. We have come to trust our intuition to lead us to the plant we need for meditation or healing. We have learned to listen with our heart and to trust the messages we receive.

We have become part of the ongoing conversation. We are not separate from the garden but a part of it. We have always been a part of the garden, but we had forgotten our place; now we remember and know the place in a deeper way.

Culpeper, Nicolas. *The Complete Herbal*. Project Gutenberg.
  https://www.gutenberg.org/files/49513/49513-h/49513-h.htm

de Bairacli Levy, Juliette, *Common Herbs For Natural Health*. Ash
  Tree Publishing, 1997.

Day, Dorothy. "Lesson 3: Class of Nonviolence." Peacecenterbooks.
  com, 7 Oct. 2014, peacecenterbooks.com/lesson-3-class-of-
  nonviolence/.

Donahue, Michelle Z. "Flowers can hear buzzing bees--and it
  makes their nectar sweeter." *National Geographic Science*, 19 June
  2019, www.nationalgeographic.com/2019/01/flowers-can-hear-
  bees-and-make-their-nectar-sweeter/.

Dunne, Daisy. "'This Beautiful Blue Planet Is Our Only Home':
  Dalai Lama Makes a 'Climate Appeal' to the World." *The
  Independent*, Independent Digital News and Media, 12 Nov. 2020,
  www.independent.co.uk/climate-change/news/dalai-lama-
  climate-crisis-appeal-world-b1721758.html.

Emerson, Ralph Waldo. "Hamatreya." 1847 Collection from Ralph
  Waldo Emerson. Wikisource, the Free Online Library, Wikimedia
  Foundation, Inc., 27 Mar. 2017, en.wikisource.org/wiki/Poems_
  (Emerson,_1847).

Emerson, Ralph Waldo. *The Complete Works*. Bartleby.com. https://
  www.bartleby.com/90/1130.html

Emoto, Masaru. *The True Power of Water: Healing and Discovering
  Ourselves*. Beyond Words Publishing, 2005.

"Holy Basil." Gaia Herbs. https://www.gaiaherbs.com/blogs/
  herbs/holy-basil

Hughes, Sylvia. "Antelope Activate the Acacia's Alarm System."
  New

Scientist, 29 Sept. 1990, www.newscientist.com/article/
  mg12717361-200-antelope-activate-the-acacias-alarm-system/.

"Nearly 600 Plant Species Have Gone Extinct In Last 250
  Years." Mongabay *Environmental News,* 17 June 2019, news.
  mongabay.com/2019/06/nearly-600-plant-species-have-
  gone-extinct-in-last-250-years/.

Phillips, Nancy, and Michael Phillips. *The Herbalist's Way*. Chelsea Green Publishing, 2005.

Rael, Joseph. *Being and Vibration: Entering the New World*. Graham, NC: Tri S Foundation, 2015.

Rael, Joseph. *Sound: Native Teaching and Visionary Art* Graham, NC: Tri S Foundation, 2009. First paperback edition, 2020.

"Slave Medicine." Monticello. https://www.monticello.org/sites/library/exhibits/lucymarks/medical/slavemedicine.html

Shakespeare, William. *Hamlet: Entire Play,* shakespeare.mit.edu/Tragedy/hamlet/full.html.

Shakespeare, William. *A Midsummer Night's Dream: Entire Play,* shakespeare.mit.edu/midsummer/full.html

Shakespeare, William. *Troilus and Cressida: Entire Play*, shakespeare.mit.edu/troilus_cressida/full.html.

Shakespeare, William. *Winter's Tale: Entire Play*, shakespeare.mit.edu/winters_tale/full.html

AUTHOR RESOURCES

Judith Brooks

judithbrooksacupuncture.com
Contact Judith for private healing consultations and herbal classes.

For further information on plant meditation and drumming
contact us at deeperintothegarden.com

Paulette Millichap

millichapbooks.com
Contact Paulette for information on books and to learn about
the Tri S Foundation, which is a 501(c)(3) nonprofit corporation
that publishes books on nature, indigenous wisdom and emerging
voices. The foundation's goal is to support indigenous wisdom in
order to enliven and renew contemporary culture.

Dodi O'Neill

dodioneill.com
oneill_designs@sonic.net
Contact Dodi for information on available art. Inquiries, questions,
and comments are welcome!

Amelia Vogler

ameliavogler.com
Contact Amelia for private intuitive healing consultations,
transformative Spiritual Development classes, and join her mailing
list for monthly meditations and new program announcements.

ADDITIONAL RESOURCES

Abdominal Therapy Collective

www.abdominaltherapycollective.com
A global community of therapists and health educators, based on
the teachings of Dr. Rosita Arvigo. Please see the website for classes
and retreats.

Rosita Arvigo

rositaarvigo.com
Contact Dr. Rosita for information on her books and classes in
Belize and the United States.

Chestnut School of Herbal Medicine: Online Herbal Programs
chestnutherbs.com
At the heart of all our teachings is our passion is for healing plants, herbal education, and medicinal gardening. We offer several online opportunities to learn, including the Herbal Medicine Making Class (150 hours), the Foraging Course (375 hours), and the Herbal Immersion Program (1,000 hours). All three classes weave together with video instruction, written lesson plans, and experiential learning.

Lyn Fairchild Hawks
Success Story Editing
success-story.lynhawks.com
Contact Lyn for information on editing fiction and nonfiction manuscripts as well as student college essays.

Joe Hollis
mountaingardensherbs.com
Contact Joe for information on seeds, plants, workshops, apprenticeships, and tours of this paradise garden in Western North Carolina specializing in native and Chinese medicinal herbs, perennial vegetables, and wild foods.

Francis Rico
shamanzone.com
Contact Francis to learn more about his online program, which offers years of shamanic training and apprenticeship in a six- month course, offering a creative realignment and orientation to "reality" that includes shamanic tools and resources.

Rainforest Remedies Ltd.
Eva & Toby Sengfelder, Belize
rainforestremediesbelize.com
Since 1992, herbal remedies ethically wildcrafted from Belize, originally formulated by Dr. Rosita Arvigo & Don Elijio Panti.
Rainforestremediesusa.com
Abigail McClam, USA distributor

Zoe Allison-Rockingbear

earthgreenmedicinelodge.com

Contact Zoe for information on divinations, Mayan Record Keeper Cards, stone earth grids and ceremonies.

United Plant Savers

unitedplantsavers.org

Their mission is to protect and conserve native medicinal plants and their habitats in the United States and Canada.

RESOURCES FOR FLOWER ESSENCES

Green Hope Farm Flower Essences

greenhopeessences.com

Located in Meriden, New Hampshire, Green Hope Farm carries collections of flower essences made throughout the world.

Floracopeia

floracopeia.com

Located in Grass Valley, California, Floracopeia carries flower essences, essential oils, and also offers a flower essence online course.

Bitterroot Botanicals

bitterrootbotanicals.com/product-page/flower-essences

Stephanie Naftal, owner of Bitterroot Botanicals, carries flower essences made from flowers in Belize and Montana.

Moonflower Medicine

Moonflowermedicine.love

Denai Grace Fuller owner of Moonflower Medicine carries flower essences made in Belize, the Pacific NW, and the Sierra Nevada Mountains.

ACKNOWLEDGEMENTS

~ Paulette ~

I would like to thank Paula Jensen for inviting me to see the world of plants through her eyes. Paula was a profound and gifted herbal teacher. She is missed by all of us who knew her.

Returning to North Carolina awakened my deep love for the land where I was born. I am grateful to my parents, Paul and Edna Pugh, who knew how to live in harmony with the natural world. I am grateful for my sister, Carolyn Hammond, and her understanding of the science of biology. I am grateful for my son, Jeff Noah, for tilling my first garden, and to Tami Noah and Bo Noah for helping me weed and tend it. I am grateful for my daughters, Donna and Kelly, who have been with me on this journey, and my son, Bob, for his technical assistance, and Cheryl and Peg for their generous support.

Judith and Paulette offer special thanks to Dodi O'Neill for her beautiful paintings, and Amelia Vogler for her heartfelt contributions of Grounding and One With All Meditation and healing plant messages. Thank you also to Francis Rico and Zoe Allison-Rockingbear for sharing their stories and teachings with us.

~ Judith ~

Many thanks to my parents, Lee and Eliot Brooks, for introducing me to gardening as a child. Gratitude for friends in North Carolina who like to go on plant walks and be in nature. Many thanks to the sisters of the Shamanic Teaching Circle; you are inspirational women.

I would like to thank the following teachers for your dedication and passion for teaching herbal medicine; Dr. Rosita Arvigo, Juliet Blankespoor, Kathleen Maier and Joe Hollis.

Will Rockingbear, Cherokee elder (1935–2013), and Grandfather Joseph Rael, thank you for sharing your wisdom and teachings with us.

The authors would like to acknowledge Judith Gadd and Kristen Kowzan for technical assistance. RJ Dobs for his patience. Carl Brune for his wonderful book design, and Lyn Hawks of *Success Story* for her helpful edits and proofreading.

We plant seeds that will flower as results in our lives, so best to remove the weeds of anger, avarice, envy and doubt, that peace and abundance may manifest for all."
DOROTHY DAY
American journalist and social activist (1897–1980)

ALL THE PAINTINGS IN THIS BOOK WERE CREATED FROM plants growing in my garden throughout the four seasons. I would start each day of painting by taking care of each plant and the plants around it. All of the plants responded to my care, creating a place for me to connect with their essence, with my own connection to the earth, and to the wild beauty.

Painting is an opportunity to simply be present in each moment with plants as my guides. It's a process of opening to the intuitive energy of creation. For me, it is a place of great freedom.

Each painting, like each plant, is a totally unique expression of the magic of life. It is a great honor and pleasure for me to be able to share this with you.

DODI O'NEILL

ABOUT THE AUTHORS

Judith Brooks resides in North Carolina and is an acupuncturist, herbalist and educator. She has travelled extensively in Central and South America, working with healers from many different traditions. Judith is an advocate for environmental awareness and plant conservation.

Paulette Millichap lives in North Carolina and was a founding partner of Council Oak Publishing. She is the Director of Tri S Foundation and publisher of Millichap Books. She celebrates over 30 years of publishing books on indigenous wisdom and nature including *In a Japanese Garden* and *Big Bluestem* with the Nature Conservancy.

Amelia Vogler is a grounding and energy medicine specialist and lives in North Carolina. She dedicates her work to sharing the Earth's messages through her healing practice, spiritual development programs, and meditations.

ABOUT THE ARTIST

Dodi O'Neill, an artist and landscape designer, says, "I'm happiest in my garden and being in nature. I've always been an artist, and painting the beauty and unique spirit of plants is my way of sharing the magic of being present in the flow of life." She lives in California.